BRUGES & GHENT

POCKET GUIDE

Walking Eye
mobile app

Discover the world's best destinations with the Insight Guides Walking Eye app, available to download for free in the App Store and Google Play.

The container app provides easy access to fantastic free content on events and activities taking place in your current location or chosen destination, with the possibility of booking, as well as the regularly-updated Insight Guides travel blog: Inspire Me. In addition, you can purchase curated, premium destination guides through the app, which feature local highlights, hotel, bar, restaurant and shopping listings, an A to Z of practical information and more. Or purchase and download Insight Guides eBooks straight to your device.

TOP 10 ATTRACTIONS

THE BEGIJNHOF
A peaceful retreat in the heart of the city.
See page 39.

ONZE-LIEVE-VROUWEKERK
One of Bruges's finest churches. See page 36.

CANALS
Cruising the waterways is a relaxing way to enjoy the historic sights. See page 122.

BELL TOWER
The 13th-century structure looms over the city.
See page 27.

GROENINGEMUSEUM
Works by Flemish masters. See page 34.

GRAVENSTEEN
A 12th-century fortress in the heart of Ghent. See page 78.

HUIS TER BEURZE
An elegant 15th-century mansion. See page 53.

STADHUIS
The gilded Gothic Town Hall. See page 29.

SINT-JANSHOSPITAAL
Discover masterpieces by the painter Hans Memling in the old hospital's church. See page 37.

BASILICA OF THE HOLY BLOOD
Stands guard over the holiest relic in Bruges. See page 30.

A PERFECT DAY

9.00am

Breakfast
For breakfast in a splendid setting, go to the Art Nouveau De Medici Sorbetière at Geldmuntstraat 9.

12.30pm

Lunch
Breydel-De Coninc (tel: 050-33 97 46; see page 104) in Breidelstraat is a good traditional restaurant. For something more sophisticated, go down Blinde-Ezelstraat and cross the canal to the Vismarkt (Fish Market) for the highly regarded seafood restaurant De Visscherie (tel: 050-33 02 12; see page 105).

2.00pm

Groeninge
Head along the canal on photogenic Rozenhoedkaai and tree-shaded Dijver, then turn left into Groeninge. If you visit only one museum in Bruges, this should be it. The collection of paintings by medieval Flemish Primitives is world-class, including Jan van Eyck, Hans Memling, Rogier van der Weyden and Gerard David, among others.

10.00am

The Markt
Stroll into the nearby Markt for a turn around the magnificent market square. Take in the Belfort and medieval buildings, then discover what 13th-century Bruges was like, inside the Historium.

11.00am

The Burg
The historic square contains the Romanesque Basiliek van het Heilig-Bloed, the lovely Gothic Stadhuis and the Baroque Proosdij.

IN BRUGES

3.00pm

Culture fix

If you fancy more culture, or you missed out on the Groeninge, cross the pretty little Boniface Bridge and continue to the Gothic Onze-Lieve-Vrouwekerk (Church of Our Lady). The church is worth visiting for its *Madonna and Child* sculpture by Michelangelo. The church's 122m (400-ft) -tall brick tower is the second-tallest of its kind in the world, and once served as an inland lighthouse for ships on their way to Bruges.

4.30pm

Towards the Begijnhof

Across the street is Sint-Janshospitaal, whose old church houses works by Hans Memling. By way of the Halve Maan brewery, you arrive at the pretty courtyard of the Unesco-listed Begijnhof.

8.00pm

Dinner

If you want to dine in this area, off the north end of the Minnewater you will find the traditional Flemish restaurant Maximiliaan van Oost-enrijk (tel: 050-33 47 23; see page 106). Alternatively, return to the Vismarkt for dinner at Huidevettershuis (tel: 050-33 95 06; see page 106), which is set within a medieval guild house.

6.00pm

The Lake of Love

Just south of the Begijnhof, the Minnewater lake can be imaginatively translated as the 'Lake of Love', though it probably takes its name from Bruges' medieval Binnen Water (Inner Harbour). On its east bank is a handsome park and the Kasteel Minnewater château. Take a stroll around here and the neighbourhood by the lake's eastern shore.

CONTENTS

INTRODUCTION

For thousands of years Belgium has been coveted, invaded and fought over by Europe's great powers. Steeped in history and legend, the country was the site of numerous bloody battles, particularly in the northern region of Flanders. Once ignored in favour of other holiday destinations, Belgium's charm is no longer a secret and its historic towns, first-class museums, hearty food, rich beers and ancient architecture are well-known. Most beautiful of all these attractions is Bruges, Europe's best-preserved medieval city and the capital of West Flanders, one of Belgium's 11 provinces.

Bruges' historic centre is contained by a 7km (4.3-mile) 'ring canal', which traces the route of the former defensive outer ramparts. A ring road follows this perimeter boundary keeping traffic away from the centre which is full of gabled houses, meandering canals, and narrow pedestrianized cobblestone streets.

The city's history is evident everywhere; in its streets and buildings, its art, culture and festivals. It has an effortless charm thanks to its compact geography and can easily be

⊘ EASY TO EXPLORE

Belgium is a compact country (less than 280km/174 miles across at its widest point), so nowhere is very far away. Most of the excursions in this guide are within a few miles of Bruges or Ghent, themselves connected by a reliable half-hour train journey. Those a little farther away are still easily accessible, thanks to the country's superb railways. In 1835 Belgium ran the first train in continental Europe, and standards are still high.

explored on foot, by bike, or even on the water.

Water forms an important part of the landscape and economy of Bruges. Canals link the city to the coast and important industrial centres in Belgium and around Europe.

Most of Belgium's population is Roman Catholic, and the virtues of community cohesion in work and play make up much of what it means to be Flemish. Tradition and family life are important, and people take their work and pleasures seriously, which explains why Belgium produces more than 450 different beers.

View from Rozenhoedkaai, where boat tours depart

Museums figure prominently in Belgium; the Belgians, at least in their civic life, have a passion for collecting and recording. Bruges shares this national characteristic, with some superb museums and galleries. It also has a rich calendar of events (see page 94), including the spectacular Procession of the Holy Blood.

Eating and drinking are mostly hearty events and form an important part of life. Belgian cuisine is justly famous throughout the world, both for its quality and its quantity; there are plenty of fine restaurants in Bruges. An intrinsic part of everyday eating is the Belgian French fry *(friet)*, which is available everywhere, and often eaten with mayonnaise. Equally ubiquitous are the exquisite Belgian chocolates you will see in mouth-watering shop displays.

A BRIEF HISTORY

Bruges has a very long and distinguished history, which considerably predates Belgium's foundation in 1830. Inhabited since the Neolithic, the region's story really begins with the Belgae, a Gallo-Germanic tribe living in northern Gaul. In the first of many centuries of occupations, Julius Caesar's armies conquered the Belgae in 54 BC.

THE KINGDOM OF THE FRANKS

The Romans withdrew from Gaul in the 5th century as the Roman Empire went into decline. Bruges was probably originally a Gallo-Roman port protected against Germanic sea-raiders by a *castellum* (fort). Much of Gaul succumbed to the Franks, who had been settling in the region for the previous two centuries. They founded their Merovingian kingdom around Tournai in the south, while the north and east regions were divided between Franks, Frisians and Saxons. The conversion to Christianity of the Frankish King Clovis in 498 led to a gradual northward spread of the new faith, which eventually converted the entire region.

A 15th-century painting of a Bruges goldsmith in his shop

In 768, the Frankish king Charlemagne established a unified kingdom. By military and diplomatic means he founded a European empire, culminating in his coronation by the Pope in 800 as Emperor of the West. On his death in 814, the empire passed to his son Louis, and on Louis' death in 840 was divided between his three sons. The division left a narrow strip of Europe, including the Low Countries (Belgium, Luxembourg and the Netherlands), sandwiched between French- and German-speaking nations.

Early record

The first recorded mention of Bruges dates from the 8th century AD, though little is known about the town's origins, except that the name possibly comes from the Vikings.

THE GOLDEN AGE OF BRUGES

The area came under the nominal rule of a succession of German and French kings, but real power was in the hands of local nobles, who tried to weaken the authority of the French and German feudal kingdoms. Some of these lords negotiated charters of rights for towns in exchange for taxes and military assistance.

Bruges began to emerge from the Dark Ages around the mid-7th century, when St Eligius preached in coastal Flanders. Chronicles of his life refer to a Frankish community called the Municipium Flandrense, which seems to have been Bruges. The first certain mention of Bruges occurs in 851 in records of monks from Ghent and by 864 the word 'Bruggia' appears on coins of Charles the Bald, king of the West Franks, to whom Flanders owed allegiance. Baldwin I, whose residence was a castle in the Burg in Bruges, is the first count of Flanders we know by name.

Baldwin built a castle at Bruges in the 9th century, and from there pursued a fierce expansionist policy to establish the county

Wealthy citizens

During what became known as the 'Joyful Entry' into Bruges in 1301, Queen Joan of Navarre marvelled at the rich apparel of the citizens: 'I thought I was the only queen, but there are hundreds more around me!'

of Flanders. In the 11th century, the succession passed to Robert the Frisian, who made Bruges his capital. The cloth towns of Flanders flourished in the 12th and 13th centuries. Ghent became the largest town in Western Europe, while Bruges had a population as large as that of medieval London, trading with the Orient, the Middle East and the rest of Europe.

International banks made Bruges their headquarters, foreign embassies located there, and the first stock exchange in Europe was founded in the city. Wool was vital to the Flemish economy: Bruges, Ghent and Ypres (Ieper) all prospered from the export of their manufactured cloth, and depended on imported wool from England. Bruges monopolised the trade in wool and, as a result, came to trade with the Hanseatic League, a powerful economic alliance of trading towns in northern Europe. The prosperity of the city reached a peak early in the 14th century.

However, tension grew between Bruges' merchants and its lords, the former tied to the English monarchy and its control over the supply of wool, the latter coerced by the hegemony of the French king. In the 13th and 14th centuries, the cloth towns of Flanders were scenes of frequent hostilities. The city walls were built during the 14th century. Four of the nine original gates survive today; powerful bastions that give some idea of past defensive strength.

The most famous conflict became known as the 'Bruges Matins'. The French king, Philip the Fair, had invaded Flanders and appointed a governor whose taxation and suppression of the powerful guilds of Bruges were so severe that on the night of 17–18 May 1302 the city revolted, led by Pieter de Coninck and Jan Breydel. The resentful rebels killed everyone they believed to be French. In the same year the French were also defeated by the Flemish, at the Battle of the Golden Spurs near Kortrijk (Courtrai).

In 1384 the region became part of the Burgundian realm. Duke Philip the Good of Burgundy became count of Flanders in 1419 and ushered in a new kind of rule. He administered his possessions in Burgundy from Bruges, and was the patron of numerous artists, including Jan van Eyck and Hans Memling; the court became renowned for its splendour. In 1429 Philip received his fiancée, Isabella of Portugal, in Bruges – the cause for a celebration of sumptuous ostentation.

Philip's successor, Charles the Bold, and his bride Margaret of York enjoyed a lavish wedding in Bruges when, it was said, the fountains spouted Burgundian wine. However, the splendour of Charles's reign did not last, and his death precipitated another French invasion of the south of the Low Countries. The people of Flanders took the opportunity to kidnap Charles's daughter Mary, forcing her in a charter to renew their civic rights (curtailed by Philip) before they would help fight the French.

Rogier van der Weyden's portrait of Philip the Good

HISTORY

THE HABSBURGS

Maximilian of Austria married Mary and assumed full control of the region immediately after her death in 1482. The era of the powerful Habsburgs had begun. The burghers of Bruges still had the nerve to incarcerate Maximilian himself briefly in 1488, exacting further promises to acknowledge their rights, but Maximilian reneged on these as soon as he was released. His grandson Charles V, born in Ghent in 1500, continued a policy of favouring Antwerp rather than the cloth towns of Flanders, despite his reception in Bruges amid great pomp and splendour in 1520. Charles' policy accelerated the economic decline of Bruges, which now had to contend with stiff competition from the cloth manufacturers in England. Bruges' death knell came when the River Zwin silted up, cutting off the town from the sea and ending its international trade; this economic slumber lasted until the 19th century.

THE REFORMATION

The Reformation was bound to have strong appeal for the merchants and people of Flanders. It stressed the rights of individuals to read and interpret the Word of God for themselves, thanks to

⊙ TRADE CENTRE

The city's early prosperity depended on its role as the chief port of Flanders, a hub for the English and Scandinavian trade. From the Roman period to the 11th century, ships sailed right into the centre of town on the River Reie. Later, seagoing ships went as far as Damme, from where smaller vessels handled canal traffic with Bruges. It was one of the most important textile centres in northwest Europe.

the invention of the printing press, and questioned the clergy's power to promulgate a worldview controlled by an alliance of State and Church. With the emergence of Luther and Calvin, pressure for reform turned into outright revolt, leading to the establishment of alternative churches. Protestantism was born.

The Low Countries were particularly receptive to new ideas, as rich merchants chafed against

Charles the Bold of Burgundy

the strictures of a rigidly hierarchical social system, while the artisanal guilds had always resented any royal authority.

Charles V's abdication in 1555 passed the Low Countries to his Catholic son, Philip II of Spain. Bloody conflict ensued. Philip and his sister Margaret harshly repressed Protestantism and tried to reinstate the authority of the Catholic Church. The 1565 harvest failure caused famine and led to the Iconoclastic Fury, when workers ran riot among the Catholic churches, sacking and destroying everything. Frightened for their own positions, the nobility sided with Margaret and Philip. In 1567 Philip sent an army to the Low Countries. The 'Pacification of Ghent', signed in 1576, instated a short-lived period of peace and freedom of worship.

A subsequent war between the Spanish and the Dutch Protestants, led by William the Silent, resulted in the Low Countries being partitioned in 1579, with the Protestant north ultimately gaining independence and the Catholic south siding with the Spanish. This partition corresponds more or less to today's border between Belgium and the Netherlands.

WAR OF THE SPANISH SUCCESSION

The Habsburg dynasty in Spain ended in 1700 when Charles II died without an heir. He had specified that Philip V of Anjou should succeed him, but the Habsburg Leopold II of Austria had other ideas. He did not like the thought of the grandson of the king of France ruling Spain, thus uniting the two kingdoms under one dynasty. He was prepared to fight for this belief and the resulting war lasted from 1701 to 1714.

The treaty that ended the war signed over the Spanish Netherlands (now Belgium) to Austrian rule. They remained in

⊘ LITERARY REVIVAL

In literature, the 19th century saw something of a flourish in Flanders. Hendrik Conscience's 1838 novel *De Leeuw van Vlaanderen (The Lion of Flanders)* re-examined the revolt against the French in 1302, when a Flemish peasant army slaughtered the flower of French chivalry at the Battle of the Golden Spurs. Georges Rodenbach's 1892 novel *Bruges-la-Morte (Dead Bruges)* resonates with the air of mystery and decay into which Bruges had declined. Charles de Coster's *The Glorious Adventures of Tijl Uilenspiegel* (1867) provided neighbouring Damme with its legendary local hero. The Catholic priest Guido Gezelle breathed new life into Flemish poetry with his volumes *Kerkhofblommen (Graveyard Flowers*, 1858), *Tijdkrans (Time's Garland*, 1893) and *Rijmsnoer (String of Rhymes*, 1897), poems dealing with nature, religion and Flemish nationalism, in a mixture of literary Dutch and West Flanders dialect.

Bruges' history is told in murals in the Stadhuis (Town Hall)

Austrian hands under Archduchess Maria Theresa, and prospered through an arrangement whereby trade was subsidised by Austria.

In 1780, Maria Theresa was succeeded by her son Joseph II. He fancied himself as a radical ruler and did institute several enlightened, secularising reforms, but his lack of consultation and his 'top-down' approach to change created widespread resentment. Sporadic rebellions occurred from 1788, and in 1790 the 'United States of Belgium' was proclaimed, winning recognition from Britain and the Netherlands. The fledgling nation was defeated a year later by the forces of the new Austrian Emperor, Leopold II.

FRENCH INVASION AND INDEPENDENCE

Despite having received military assistance from a Belgian contingent against the Austrians in 1792, the army of revolutionary France invaded Belgium and the Netherlands two years later and occupied the annexed countries for the next 20 years – though not without some benefit to Belgium. The country was divided into a number of *départements* along French lines, while important and unjust aspects of Church, State, and taxation were reformed or abolished. There was also rapid subsidised industrialisation, with France being the main market for Belgian manufactured goods.

However, Belgium's people resented occupation. Rebellions broke out from 1798 onwards. Following Napoleon's final defeat at the Battle of Waterloo in 1815, the Congress of Vienna perpetuated Belgium's subjugation by passing control to the Dutch House of Orange. It was not until the revolution in 1830 that an autonomous free Belgian state was created. In 1831, the London Conference recognised the independence of Belgium and established a constitutional monarchy. Leopold I was awarded the crown.

ARMAGEDDON – TWICE

Throughout the 19th century, Belgium modernised, immersing itself in the Industrial Revolution. Slowly, Bruges was being rediscovered by British travellers on their way to the site of the Battle of

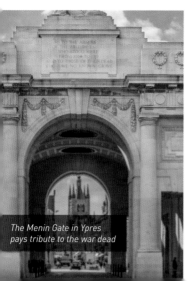

The Menin Gate in Ypres pays tribute to the war dead

Waterloo. Ghent revived, becoming a major economic centre. Yet tensions between different linguistic groups became more obvious as social difficulties failed to be resolved. In need of a scapegoat, the predominantly Dutch-speaking (and increasingly prosperous) north agitated for independence from the (French-speaking) Walloon south. Instead of attending to the problems of his country, the new king of Belgium, Leopold II (1865–1909) devoted most of his time to personal interests. In 1909 his nephew succeeded him, as Albert I.

> **Famine in Flanders**
>
> In the mid-19th century, living conditions for working people were appalling, aggravated by a dreadful famine in Flanders from 1845 to 1848. Almost half the population of Bruges was dependent on charity.

During Albert's reign, World War I gripped Belgium for four years. In 1914, the German army invaded, despite the country's neutrality, forcing the king to move to a narrow remaining strip of unoccupied Belgium. His resistance to the invaders gained him international renown as the 'Soldier King'.

The war's northern front extended roughly diagonally across the country, with the most infamous, and bloodiest, of battles taking place around Ypres (Ieper) in western Flanders. The defeat of Germany won Belgium considerable reparations and some new territory.

It might have been expected that the experience of war would draw the nation together, especially when King Albert proclaimed a series of reforms meant to improve equality between the Flemish and the Walloons. However, fascism was already working its way through both communities and they grew more antagonistic. In 1940, the German army marched into Belgium, occupying it in just three weeks.

Bruges suffered little damage, though its new canal had to be repaired extensively.

A resistance movement formed, including an underground network to protect Belgium's Jews. However, the behaviour of the king, Leopold III, who was eager to accommodate the invaders, caused much controversy after the war as Belgium sought to rebuild itself. In 1950, the people voted by a narrow margin to ask the king home from exile, but Leopold decided to abdicate in favour of his son, Baudouin I.

REGIONALISATION

After forming Benelux, an economic union with the Netherlands and Luxembourg, Belgium went on to join the European Economic Community in 1957, with Brussels the seat of the organisation. Though this has ensured that Belgium is internationally recognised as the home of European bureaucracy, it has nevertheless retained its own distinct national character.

The country finally divested itself of the Congo (now the Democratic Republic of Congo) in 1960. Internal political events since the end of World War II have been dominated by continuing friction between the Flemish and Walloons. In 1977, three federal regions were established – Wallonia, Flanders and Brussels – in an attempt to ease the tensions between the groups by giving them greater self-determination. In 1989, regional governments were created, each with responsibility for all policy except matters concerning social security, defence and foreign affairs. A new constitution was adopted in 1994, establishing Belgium as a federal state.

In practice, visitors will see little sign of intercommunity tension and the unifying presence of King Philippe and the royal family helps to preserve a sense of nationhood.

HISTORICAL LANDMARKS

58–51BC Roman conquest of Gaul, including present-day Belgium.

AD498 Conversion to Christianity of Frankish King Clovis.

768 Charlemagne's unified Frankish kingdom is established.

Early 800s Castle (Burg) built at Bruges.

851 First certain mention of Bruges.

864 Baldwin becomes first known Count of Flanders.

11th century Silting cuts off Bruges's access to the sea.

1134 Storm creates Zwin inlet, restoring Bruges's access to the sea.

1150 Count Thierry returns from Crusades with Relic of the Holy Blood.

1302 Bruges Matins and Battle of the Golden Spurs.

1384 Flanders becomes part of Burgundian kingdom.

1419 Philip the Good of Burgundy becomes count of Flanders.

1482 Habsburg reign begins with Maximilian of Austria.

1520 Silting closes Zwin inlet, cutting off access to the sea again.

1555 Charles V abdicates; Philip II of Spain succeeds.

1567–79 Religious wars in the southern Low Countries.

1790 Proclamation of United States of Belgium.

1794 French invade and occupy country for 20 years.

1815 Napoleon defeated at Waterloo; Congress of Vienna.

1830 Belgian revolution and independence.

1914–18 World War I; Germans invade neutral Belgium.

1940 Nazi Germany occupies Belgium during World War II.

1977 Establishment of Flanders as one of three federal Belgian regions.

1993 Albert II becomes king of the Belgians.

2002 The Concertgebouw concert and opera hall opens in the city.

2008 Bruges is the setting for the hit black-comedy film *In Bruges*.

2013 King Philippe assumes the throne after the abdication of his father Albert II. Socialist Renaat Landuyt becomes Bruges' mayor.

2014 Beer Museum opens in Bruges.

2016 35 people are killed in three coordinated suicide attacks carried out by the so-called Islamic State in Brussels; the number of tourists visiting Bruges falls 16.5 percent.

The red roofs of central Bruges

WHERE TO GO

Bruges is made for walking: it is very compact, with attractions clearly signposted. It has been dubbed the 'Venice of the North', and while this comparison is unfair to both places, it should come as no surprise that canal cruises are one of the best ways of viewing the city: central Bruges has 10km (6 miles) of canals, and 4km (2.5 miles) of them are accessible by boat tour.

The capital of West Flanders, Bruges is Belgium's most popular tourist destination, so be prepared for large crowds in the summer. This doesn't diminish the city's charm, but it does mean queues for the main sights and art galleries may be longer, so try to plan in advance. Many visitors arrive for the day by bus, so if you're staying overnight you can wander in peace come evening. Ambling through the city's narrow streets and open market-places is a pleasure, with new views around each corner – there is always something else to delight the eye and fire the imagination.

Paradoxically, it was Bruges' five centuries of economic decline that preserved the buildings we now enjoy; there was never any money to demolish and rebuild. The badly dilapidated city was 'discovered' by visitors in the 19th century. In the quieter residential quarters you can still sense what it must have been like to walk through the

Bruges Museum Pass

If you plan on visiting several of the city's museums, it is worth buying the Bruges Museum Pass (www.visitbruges.be). Valid for three consecutive days, it costs €20/15 (over 25/12–25) and grants free entry to 14 museums. There is also the Musea Brugge Card, which is valid for a year and costs €30/40 (1 person/2 persons).

The belfry of Belfort-Hallen

streets of a forgotten town, your footsteps ringing on the cobblestones, while church bells chime and a horse's hooves echo from a nearby street.

One of the first things to strike visitors is the harmonious appearance of the architecture. The characteristic stepped gables of the houses may be a bit worn with age, but this only adds to their charm. You will notice that most buildings are of brick, with their shutters and woodwork painted in traditional Bruges red. Bruges is now so beautifully restored that you may briefly find yourself yearning for something less perfect just by way of contrast; Belgians themselves describe the place as an outdoor museum.

Enjoy the route suggested here, but also take the time to improvise and discover the city on your own, perhaps simply following the canals, or tracing the path of the city walls with their big, imposing gates. Horse-drawn carriages and bicycle taxis can also be hired.

Our walk begins at the **Markt ❶**, Bruges' main square. Before you set off, take time to look around. This may be the 21st century, but not much has changed since some of the civic buildings and houses that you can see were constructed; it's not hard to imagine what the place would have looked like in the city's bustling golden age, when merchants flocked here from all over Europe.

SOUTH FROM THE MARKT

On the southeast side of the square, dominating the skyline, is the magnificent complex of brick buildings known as the **Belfort-Hallen** (Bell Tower and Covered Market; daily 9.30am–6pm, last entry 5pm). One of the first priorities of any visitor is to ignore the 1m (3ft) lean of the 83m (272ft) belfry and climb its 366 steps for a breath-taking view of the town and surrounding countryside. The best times to climb it are early morning or late afternoon. The belfry dates from the 13th century, when Bruges was at the height of its prosperity, but the final storey (with the clock) is 15th-century. The second floor houses a treasury where the town seal and charters were kept safely behind intricate Romanesque grilles (built in 1292), each requiring nine separate keys to open them.

You may already have heard the 47-bell carillon, which weighs 27 tons and hangs in the tower above. The belfry is an excellent landmark when you're finding your way around. The covered market and courtyard, also dating from the 13th century, would have been crammed with traders, the air heavy with the scent of spices brought by Venetian merchants. A canal lay below the covered market, which was used for the loading and unloading of goods. City statutes were announced from the balcony over the market entrance.

The neo-Gothic **Provinciaal Hof,** located on the east side of the Markt, houses the West Flanders provincial government (not open to visitors) and beside it is the **Historium** (www.historium.

Bruges Matins

At the centre of the Markt is a 19th-century monument to the heroes of the Bruges Matins (see page 14), Pieter De Coninck and Jan Breydel. Stained green with age, they still look suitably determined.

be; daily 10am–6pm), an interactive museum depicting life in the Middle Ages.

The **Craenenburg**, on the opposite side of the square, now an atmospheric café-brasserie, was where the Habsburg Crown Prince Maximilian of Austria was briefly imprisoned in 1488. The future emperor, understandably disgruntled, did his best ever afterwards to promote trade through Antwerp at the expense of Bruges (see page 16).

On the same side of the square, at the corner of Sint-Amandsstraat, is a beautiful 15th-century brick building, **Huis Bouchoute**. Restored in 1995 to its original brick Gothic, including removing later rooftop crenulations, this house hosted the exiled English King Charles II in 1656–7. The roof-mounted octagonal compass and weathervane (1682) allowed Bruges' merchants to judge their ships' chances of entering or leaving the port.

THE BURG

A stroll down Breidelstraat, in the southeast corner of the Markt (next to the Halle), takes you past narrow De Garre, the shortest street in Bruges; if you need refreshment, there's a cosy 100-beer bar at the end, the Staminee de Garre. Alternatively, visit the nearby Brugs Biermuseum. on Breidel-straat 3 (Bruges Beer Museum; daily 10am–6.30pm), which tells the story of Belgian beer and allows visitors to taste some of the best local brands. Breidelstraat leads to the **Burg ❷**, one of Europe's finest medieval squares, named after the castle built by Baldwin the Iron Arm.

Which building in the square is the most splendid? It's a hard choice. On the corner of Breidelstraat and the Burg is the ornate Baroque **Proosdij** (Deanery), formerly the palace of the bishops of Bruges, dating from 1666. Its parapet is lined with urns and topped with a handsome female personification of justice armed with sword and scales. The building stands on the site of the demolished Sint-Donaaskerk (St Donatian's), a Carolingian-style church built around 950.

The **Stadhuis** (Town Hall; daily 9.30am–5pm) on the south side of the Burg was constructed between 1376 and 1420. It is one of the oldest town halls in Belgium and a Gothic mas-

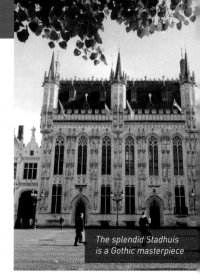

The splendid Stadhuis is a Gothic masterpiece

terpiece, its delicately traced windows framed within pilasters topped with octagonal turrets. If you stand close to the building its statues and spiral chimneys seem to be curving down over you, and the detailing of the sandstone facade becomes even more impressive. The statues on the facade are of the counts of Flanders.

The exterior of the Stadhuis promises great things and the interior of the magnificent town hall will certainly not let you down. Bluestone stairs lead from the flag-draped entrance hall to the first-floor Gothic Hall, a splendid room that witnessed the first meeting of the States General, set up in 1464 by the dukes of Burgundy to regulate provincial contributions to the treasury. The vaulted oak ceiling, with its long pendant keystones at the junctions of the arches, is richly decorated in tones of brown, black, maroon and gold, surrounding painted scenes from the New Testament.

The murals depict important events in the city's history. The De Vriendt brothers painted them in 1905 after the original 1410 wall decorations were lost. The small, delicate balcony near the entrance door was for the town pipers and other musicians. The hall is used for civic ceremonies, receptions and weddings. An adjoining room displays old coins, documents and other artefacts relating to the history of Bruges.

To the right of the Stadhuis as you face it is the small gilded entrance to the **Basiliek van het Heilig-Bloed** (Basilica of the Holy Blood; daily 9.30am–12pm, 2–5.30pm). Its three-arched facade was completed by 1534, making it a mere youth in comparison with the Stadhuis. Its ornate stone carvings and gilded statues of angels, knights and their ladies stand below two closely adjoining and strangely Islamic-looking towers of great delicacy. The interior of the basilica is divided into two chapels, a 12th-century Romanesque lower chapel and a Gothic upper chapel, providing a dramatic contrast in styles. The lower chapel is a study in shadows, with austere, unadorned lines, uncompromising Romanesque pillars, and little decoration except for a relief carving over an interior doorway depicting the baptism of St Basil (an early Church Father). St Basil's relics were brought back from Palestine by Robert II, count of Flanders. The faded carving is child-like in style, its naivety emphasised by the two mismatched columns supporting it.

Ascension Day

On Ascension Day every year, the holy relic is carried through Bruges in the famous Heilig-Bloed Processie (Procession of the Holy Blood), the most important of West Flanders' festivals. The venerated phial is transported in a flamboyant gold and silver reliquary that is normally kept in the treasury off the chapel.

Access to the upper chapel is through a beautiful late-Gothic doorway. Ascending by a broad, elegant 16th-century spiral staircase, you can enter the upper chapel beneath the organ case. The lines of the chapel have been spoiled somewhat by over-enthusiastic 19th-century decoration and murals, but the greater impression is of warmth and richness. The ceiling looks like an upturned boat and the

The Basilica of the Holy Blood

room is flooded with a golden light. The bronze-coloured pulpit is a curious sight, bearing a remarkable resemblance to a cored and stuffed tomato.

In a small side chapel you will find the holy relic from which the church derives its name. Flemish knight Dirk of Alsace returned from the Second Crusade in the Holy Land in 1149 and is said to have brought with him a crystal phial believed to contain some drops of Christ's blood. Once venerated all over medieval Europe, it is still brought out each Friday for the faithful. The dried blood turned to liquid at regular intervals for many years, an event declared by Pope Clement V to be a miracle. The phial is stored in a richly and rather heavily ornate silver tabernacle presented by the archdukes of Spain in 1611. It is carried in procession through the streets every year on Ascension Day.

Opposite the basilica, the **Landhuis van het Brugse Vrije** (Liberty of Bruges Palace) is an early 18th-century neoclassical building on the site of an older structure that used to house the law courts: at the rear of the building overlooking the canal are the remains of an attractive 16th-century facade.

Part of the palatial building now houses the **Brugse Vrije** (Liberty of Bruges; daily 9.30am–12.30pm, 1.30–5pm), with an entrance at Burg 11. The museum has one main exhibit, the **Renaissancezaal** (Renaissance Hall), the Liberty's restored council chamber. The great black marble and oak Renaissance 'Emperor Charles' chimneypiece, designed by the painter Lanceloot Blondeel in tribute to Charles V, was started in 1528 and finished in 1531. This is one of the most memorable artworks in Bruges: the carving is on a monumental scale, covering an entire wall and joining the ceiling with carved tendrils and caskets. A statue of Charles in full armour, wearing the emblem of the Order of the Golden Fleece, is in the centre. Forty-six coats of arms and ribbons of wood also appear on it. Among many of the scenes, the design depicts the defeat of the French at Pavia and the biblical story of Susanna and the Elders. The intricate craftsmanship of the piece is superb and quite overwhelming, but the handholds for gentlemen to use while drying their boots are the sort of domestic touch everyone remembers.

Adjoining this building is the statue-laden, Renaissance-style **Oude Civiele Griffie** (Old Registrar's House), completed in 1537. Note how the sinuously curved and scrolled gables contrast with the older, linear step gables of most of the architecture in Bruges.

AROUND VISMARKT

Wander through the Renaissance arch joining the Oude Civiele Griffie and the Stadhuis, and follow Blinde Ezelstraat (Blind Donkey Street) across the bridge until you reach the colonnaded **Vismarkt ❸** (Fishmarket; Tue–Sat 8am–1.30pm). Built

Canal cruises are a perfect way to view the city

in 1821, the market sells fresh fish from the North Sea along with a variety of craft items. Lining both sides of the canal are some pretty little streets.

At Groenerei (left at the bridge) is the 1634 **Godshuis De Pelikaanhuis** (Pelican House). Easily identified by its pelican emblem over the doorway, this was once a hospital, or almshouse. Such almshouses can be found all over Bruges: the city's guilds and wealthy merchants built them to shelter the sick, elderly and poor. They are usually low, whitewashed cottages like the ones in Zwarteleertouwerstraat (take the last right turn in Groenerei).

Back behind the Vismarkt, you can wander through Huidenvettersplein (Tanners' Square), which has become something of a growth area for cafés and restaurants. The turreted **Huidevettershuis** (Tanners' Guild Hall), built in 1630, is now a restaurant.

Beyond the square, **Rozenhoedkaai** (Rosary Quay) is one of the places from where boat tours depart; do stop to enjoy the view from the quay. The River Dijver, a branch of the Reie, begins at **Sint-Jan Nepomucenusbrug** (St John of Nepomuk Bridge). A statue portrays the good man himself, appropriately the patron saint of bridges. The tree-lined riverbank is the site of a weekend antiques market; the river passes superb old houses and crosses the canal into Gruuthusestraat. On the left is a complex of museums: the Groeninge, the Brangwyn and the Gruuthuse.

THE GROENINGE MUSEUM

The **Groeningemuseum** ❹ (Tue–Sun 9.30am–5pm) contains some of the great works of the Flemish Primitives, including Van Eyck's portrait of his supercilious-looking wife Margareta, which is so typical of the painter's incredible realism; and Bosch's deeply disturbing *Last Judgement*, with the fires of hell ablaze. The *Judgement of Cambyses*, painted by Gerard David in 1498, depicts the judicial skinning of a corrupt judge while detached onlookers coolly observe the proceedings.

Other treasures include Memling's glorious *Moreel Triptych* depicting St Christopher with portraits in the side panels, and his

'Madonna and Child' by Jan Van Eyck, 1436

St John Altarpiece. In addition, there are magnificent portraits by Hugo van der Goes, Rogier van der Weyden and Petrus Christus, as well as paintings by unknown masters, many of them depicting detailed views of the city.

Welsh war artist

Frank Brangwyn was a disciple of the Arts and Crafts Movement and apprentice to its greatest exponent, William Morris, before becoming a war artist in World War I.

However, the greatest work in the museum is Van Eyck's *Madonna and Child with Canon Joris van der Paele*, where the textures and folds of the clothing and carpets are reproduced with breath-taking effect. There is also work from later periods, including a landscape by James Ensor, enigmatic work by René Magritte, and some pieces by Flemish Expressionists – but the early Flemish artists steal the show.

THE ARENTSHUIS

The **Arentshuis** (Tue–Sun 9.30am–5pm) at Dijver 16 contains the extensive art collection of Sir Frank Brangwyn, a Welsh artist born in Bruges in 1867 who bequeathed his work to the city when he died in 1956. In addition to his realistic paintings depicting industrial life in the docks and factories, Brangwyn was known for colourful travel scenes. Also on display are items of furniture, prints and rugs that he designed. Temporary exhibitions are held on the ground floor.

THE GRUUTHUSE MUSEUM

In the courtyard at the rear of the Arentshuis you can see Rik Poot's sculptures of the *Four Horsemen of the Apocalypse*, a scary combination of robotic armour and animal skeletons. A hump-backed bridge connects the courtyard to the

Gruuthusemuseum ❺ (www.visitbruges.be; closed for renovation until 2018), so called because the original owners had rights to tax the *gruut* used by brewers (the herbs, spices and plants used in brewing before the introduction of hops).

The building itself is one of the museum's best exhibits; a splendid **mansion** of red brick. Built in the 15th century, it has twice sheltered fugitive English kings: both Edward IV and Charles II stayed here, in 1471 and 1656 respectively. The museum has an exceptional collection of lacework, tapestries and musical instruments, including a delicate spinet..

ONZE-LIEVE-VROUWEKERK

The exterior of **Onze-Lieve-Vrouwekerk** ❻ (Church of Our Lady; Tue–Sun 9.30am–12.30, 1.30–5pm) is a mix of different styles and is slightly forbidding. More interesting is the interior, which is filled with religious artworks and treasures. Chief among them is the *Madonna and Child* (1504) by Michelangelo, originally intended for Siena Cathedral and the only one of his works to travel outside Italy during his lifetime. It was brought to Bruges by a Flemish merchant called Jan van Moeskroen. The Madonna is a subdued, preoccupied figure, while the infant leans nonchalantly on her knee.

There are some fine paintings here by Pieter Pourbus (*Last Supper* and *Adoration of the Shepherds*) and Gerard David (*Transfiguration*), but, after the Michelangelo, it is the chancel area that holds most interest. Here you can see the **tombs** of Charles the Bold and his daughter Mary of Burgundy, fine examples of, respectively, Renaissance and late Gothic carving. Both are richly decorated with coats of arms linked with floral motifs in copper-gilt gold, reds and blues. The figures themselves, which have domestic details like the pet dogs at Mary's feet, are also in copper gilt. Whether or not Charles and Mary are actually buried here is a matter of some dispute. Charles died in battle in Nancy in 1477 and it was difficult to identify the body. Mary (who died in a riding accident at the age of 25, bringing to a close the 100-year reign of the House of Burgundy) may be buried among a group of poly-chromed tombs in the choir that were discovered in 1979. You can see the frescoed tombs through windows in the floor and mirrors in front of the sarcophagi.

Elsewhere in the church, you will find the funerary chapel of Pieter Lanchals (see page 40), containing frescoed tombs in maroon and black; and Van Dyck's starkly atmospheric painting of Christ on the Cross. The splendid wooden gallery overlooking the chancel belongs to the adjacent Gruuthuse mansion (see page 36) and dates from the 15th century.

SINT-JANSHOSPITAAL
Opposite the church is **Sint-Janshospitaal ❼** (St

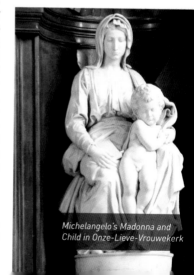

Michelangelo's Madonna and Child in Onze-Lieve-Vrouwekerk

John's Hospital; Tue–Sun 9.30am–5pm). Constructed in the 12th century, and now below street level, this is the oldest building in Bruges. In what were once the hospital wards, there is an exhibition of historical documents and alarming surgical instruments. The 17th-century pharmacy has a carved relief showing patients sleeping two to a bed. The hospital was still functioning in the 19th century, and there is a strong sense of tradition, enhanced by an informative visitor centre.

The old hospital church is largely devoted to six masterpieces by the Flemish master Hans Memling. Each of the exhibited works displays Memling's captivating attention to detail and mastery of realism. It is impossible to pick the 'best', but probably the most famous is the detailed *Reliquary of St Ursula*, one of the greatest art treasures in the country. Commissioned by two sisters who worked in the church, the reliquary is in the form of a miniature Gothic chapel with Memling's painted panels in the positions of the windows.

The *Mystic Marriage of St Catherine* includes St John the Evangelist and St John the Baptist, patron saints of the hospital: it has been suggested that saints Catherine and Barbara are portraits of Mary of Burgundy and Margaret of York. A painting by Jan Beerbloch depicts the

The canal frontage of Sint-Janshospitaal

relaxed standards of hospital hygiene: nurses sweep the floors while dogs wander the wards.

AROUND MARIASTRAAT

If you head south along Mariastraat and look left along Nieuwe Gentweg, there are some typical white almshouses that have gardens open to the public. The next turning on the right is Walstraat, a peaceful street of delightful 16th- and 17th-century gabled houses where lacemaking is still practised (outside on warm days).

If your thirst for culture is overtaken by a thirst for something else, a short stroll will bring you to **Brouwerij De Halve Maan** (The Half Moon; www.halvemaan.be; daily 11am–4pm; guided tours) at Walplein 26. Belgium is well known for its many hundreds of beers, and Bruges beers are exceptionally good. De Halve Maan has been brewing in the city since 1564 and today produces a light, highly fermented local beer called Straffe Hendrik (Strong Henry, after its high-alcohol content). Brugse Zot beer joined it in 2005. The 45-minute tour of the museum will reveal how it is done, and includes an ascent to the roof for a good view over the gables of central Bruges. The building is suffused with a sweet smell from the brewing process. At the end of the visit, each visitor gets a drink in the congenial bar, lined with every conceivable shape of beer bottle.

THE BEGIJNHOF

South of the church along Mariastraat, follow the signposts to the **Begijnhof** ❽. Belgium is famous for its many residences for tertiary religious orders, which were for unmarried or widowed women (known as Beguines) who wished to live under religious rule without having to commit themselves to the full vows of a nun. The women cared for the sick and made a living by lacemaking.

The **Prinselijk Begijnhof ten Wijngaarde** (Princely Beguin-age of the Vineyard; daily 6.30am–6.30pm; free) was founded in 1245 by Margaret of Constantinople and remained a Beguine residence until its conversion into a Benedictine convent in the 20th century. Nuns wear the traditional clothes of the Beguines and maintain some of their predecessors' customs. The convent is one of the most attractive Beguine residences. Reached by a bridge over the canal and through an arch, it comprises a circle of white, 17th-century houses set around a courtyard of grass and trees that comes alive with daffodils each spring. In a city replete with picturesque views, this is one of the most photographed places. You can visit the Begijnhof's church, **Onze-Lieve-Vrouw van Troost van Spermalie** (Our Lady of Consolation of Spermalie), when the nuns are having a service. Alternatively, the **Begijnhuisje** (Beguine House; Mon–Sat 10am–5pm, Sun 2.30–5pm), one of the Beguines' cottages, is still largely in its 17th-century condition. A stroll around the tree-shaded cloister garden, a blaze of colour in spring and summer, is a delight.

Around the Begijnhof the street layout is as it was in the 17th century, so take time to wander around and enjoy the views. This is also where the hard-working carriage horses of Bruges

Why the swans?

There have been swans on Minnewater, so the story goes, since 1488 when Emperor Maximilian was imprisoned in Bruges and his councillor, Pieter Lan-chals, was beheaded. Lan-chals' coat of arms featured a swan, and the emperor ordered that swans be kept on the canals of Bruges for evermore, as a reminder of the city's dreadful crime.

stop to enjoy a well-earned rest mid-tour, with a drink of water pumped from a horse's head statue.

MINNEWATER

The picturesque and understandably popular park and lake of **Minnewater** ❾ (Lake of Love) lie to the south of Walplein and Wijngaardplein. The lake was originally the inner harbour of Bruges, before the Zwin inlet silted up and cut off the city from the sea; you

A nun in the Begijnhof

can still see the 15th-century Sashuis (Lock House). Beyond the Sashuis, the tower on the right is the Poertoren (Powder Tower), a remnant of old fortifications. On the east side of the basin is leafy **Minnewater Park**, in which stands **Kasteel Minnewater** (Minnewater Castle).

Take Wijngaardstraat and turn right into Noordstraat, to the **Godshuis de Vos** (1713). You can look over the wall into the courtyard of this enchanting almshouse, where the original eight little houses are now converted to six.

KATELIJNESTRAAT

Turn left into Arsenalstraat and left again into Katelijnestraat, to the **Stedelijke Academie voor Schone Kunsten** (Municipal Fine Arts Academy), housed in a former Beghard Monastery at No. 86. These male counterparts to the beguines established themselves here in the 13th century. The complex

The 'Lake of Love' – picturesque Minnewater

became a school for poor children in 1513 and took on its present role in 1891. Also in Katelijnestraat, at No. 43, is the **Diamantmuseum** ⑩ (Diamond Museum; www.diamond museum.be; daily 10.30am–5.30pm). The museum documents the history of diamond polishing, a technique thought to have been invented by the Bruges goldsmith Lodewijk van Berquem in the mid-15th century. There is a reconstruction of van Berquem's workshop, some examples of tools and machinery used in diamond polishing, plus models, paintings and rare rock samples. Demonstrations further illustrate the technique (Sat–Sun 12.15pm and 1.15pm, and daily May, Jul, Aug; other months Mon–Fri 12.15pm).

Katalijnestraat connects with Nieuwe Gentweg, where you can visit a cluster of attractive *godshuizen* (almshouses): **De Meulenaere** (dating from 1613); **Sint-Jozef** (St Joseph; 1674); and, around the corner in Drie Kroezenstraat,

Onze-Lieve-Vrouw van de Zeven Weeën (Our Lady of the Seven Sorrows, founded in 1654).

WEST FROM THE MARKT

Go along Steenstraat, a beautiful street lined with gabled guild houses, headquarters of the trading and craft guilds that contributed so much to the medieval city's life. There is the Bakers' Guild House at No. 19, the Stonemasons' Guild House at No. 25, the Joiners' Guild House at No. 38, and the Shoemakers' Guild House at No. 40. All of these now house either shops or banks. This brings you to **Simon Stevinplein**, and its bronze sculpture of the Bruges mathematician and scientist Simon Stevin, who fled from his native city around 1580 during the anti-Protestant persecutions carried out by its Spanish rulers. He later lived and worked in Holland. The square was laid out in 1819 and the statue, which depicts Stevin holding a set of dividers in one hand and a manuscript in the other, dates from 1847.

If you make a short detour south of Simon Stevinplein to Oude Burg, you will find the **Hof van Watervliet**. The 16th-century buildings have been much restored, but are still of interest. Former residents included the humanist scholar Erasmus and the exiled Charles II of England.

Further along Steenstraat you will come to **Sint-Salvators-kathedraal** ⓫ (Saint Saviour's Cathedral; www.sintsalvator.be; Mon–Fri 10am–1pm, 2–5.30pm, Sat 10am–1pm, 2–3.30pm, Sun 11.30–noon, 2–5pm; worshippers only during

Zandfeesten

On a Saturday morning 't Zand Square hosts one of Europe's biggest street markets. The vast Zandfeesten (Zand Festival) flea market is also held here a few times each year.

services). The oldest parish church in Bruges, it has been a cathedral since 1834, replacing the city centre cathedral destroyed by the French in the late 18th century. Parts of the building date from the 12th and 13th centuries, though the church was originally founded in the 10th century. The Gothic interior is quite Spartan and curiously unfocused in design, but the choir stalls and the Baroque rood screen showing God the Father are worth a look. The cathedral treasury (Mon–Fri, Sun 2pm–close), is located off the right transept. Specialising in liturgical objects, it is worth visiting for its Flemish paintings, including work by Dirk Bouts and Pieter Pourbus.

AROUND 'T ZAND SQUARE

Continuing along Zuidzandstraat, you come to bustling **'t Zand** ⑫, a square lined with numerous hotels and cafés. Notice the fountain and groups of modern sculpture by Stefaan Depuydt and Livia Canestraro. The four female figures in *Bathing Women* symbolise Antwerp, Bruges, Kortrijk and Ghent; *Landscape of Flanders* is an abstract representation of the region's flat terrain; *The Cyclists* is an expression of youth and hope for the future; and *The Fishermen* represents Bruges' ancient ties with the sea.

Along Boeveriestraat from 't Zand, at Klokstraat, is the **Kapucijnenkerk** (Capuchin Church), the church of a Capuchin monastery built here in 1869 to replace an earlier one in what is now 't Zand Square. The monastery was demolished to make way for the city's original railway station, which has itself vanished. On the left side of Boeveriestraat stands the Benedictine **Sint-Godelieve Abdij** (St Godelina Abbey). The nuns first moved into the city in the 16th century and established themselves here in 1623. Behind its brick facade is a wide green lawn. Across the street, you will find the grounded **Dumery-Klok** (Dumery Bell). This used to hang in the belfry above the Markt and was placed here as a memento of the 18th-century Dumery Bell Foundry that once stood here. Also on this street and around the neighbourhood are the *godshuizen* (almshouses) **Van Campen** (1436), **Van Peenen** (1621), **Gloribus** (1634), **Sucx** (1436), and **De Moor** (1480).

The park that now occupies the line of the city's medieval wall and moat leads north, past the **Oud Waterhuis** (Old Water House; 1394), part of the city's water distribution system, which drew supplies from the canals and other sources. Continuing north brings you to the **Smedenpoort** (Marshal's Gate), one of the four fortified city gates that survive of the nine that were once dotted around the now mostly vanished city walls. Dating from 1368 with additions from the 17th century, it is a powerful-looking piece of military engineering.

Take Smedenstraat back towards 't Zand and the Markt. A short diversion into Kreupelenstraat lets you visit the

Onze-Lieve-Vrouw-van-Blindekenskapel (Chapel of Our Lady of the Blind; daily 9am–5pm). This bright and simple 17th-century church has a carved pulpit from 1659 and a gilded 14th-century statue of the *Madonna and Child* above a side altar. Every 15 August, on the feast of the Assumption, a procession leaves from here and wends its way to the church of Onze-Lieve-Vrouw van de Potterie (Our Lady of the Pottery) in the northeast of the city (see page 55). A further diversion, this time along the handsome Speelmansrei canal, leads to the little Gothic **Speelmanskapel** (Minstrels' Church; 1421). The nearby **Stadspark Sebrechts** stands on land once occupied by the nuns of the Sint-Elisabethklooster, which was dissolved in 1784. In summer the park becomes an open-air museum of modern sculpture.

Nearby Noordzandstraat is the site of the **Prinsenhof** ⓭ (Prince's Court), once the residence of dukes and duchesses of Burgundy, and later of Habsburg emperors and empresses. During the Burgundian period it was the ultimate in pomp and splendour. When Charles the Bold was engaged in his ill-starred quest to make Burgundy a third continental power, alongside France and Germany, the Prinsenhof was a radiant nucleus, and Bruges the largest, richest and most powerful city north of the Alps. Burgundian-era highlights took place in this setting. Philip the Good celebrated his marriage to

Golden Fleece

Philip the Good founded the chivalric Order of the Golden Fleece in 1430, on the occasion of his wedding to Isabella of Portugal. Its knights formed the cream of Burgundian high society, but according to a French report published in 1620, the Golden Fleece referred not to the mythological quest of Jason and the Argonauts, but to the lustrous hair of one of Philip's mistresses.

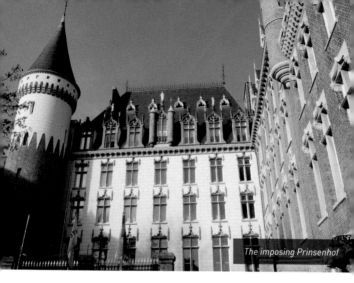

The imposing Prinsenhof

Isabella of Portugal in 1430 and Charles the Bold his marriage to Margaret of York in 1468, with banquets that made the term 'Burgundian' a byword for lavishness. Duchess Mary gave birth to Philip the Handsome here in 1479, and in 1482 she died here, as had Philip the Good in 1467.

Not much survives of the 14th-century palace, yet the Prinsenhof is still imposing. Constantly remodelled throughout the Burgundian century, the palace was put up for sale in 1631 and purchased in 1662 by the Order of St Francis, for a convent. In 1794, the nuns departed for Delft, ahead of the incoming French Revolutionary army, and the property was sold again. In 1888, another group of nuns took possession, this time the French Dames de la Retraite. A century later the palace was sold to a private concern and used as a centre for exhibitions, conferences and concerts. It now houses the Hotel Dukes' Palace.

In little Muntplein Square is a small equestrian statue, *Flandria Nostra*, of Mary of Burgundy riding side-saddle. The daughter of Charles the Bold, she died in 1482 at the age of 25, after falling from her horse while hunting. She now occupies a sarcophagus in the Church of Our Lady (see page 36).

Just before re-entering the Markt, at Geldmuntstraat 9, you pass the Art Nouveau shop front of the **De Medici Sorbetière.**

NORTH FROM THE MARKT

The city north of the Markt used to be the home and business premises of the merchants of medieval Bruges, for it was common practice to live and work in the same building. The avenues of elegant houses from this period are punctuated with grandiose mansions dating from the 18th century, and the canals here meet and diverge in broad highways of water. It is no wonder that many visitors regard this as their favourite part of the city.

JAN VAN EYCKPLEIN

Just a few minutes' walk north from the Markt along Vlamingstraat is **Jan van Eyckplein ⑭** and adjoining Spiegelrei. Bruges has many former harbours, and this one was the busiest of them all; the canal that terminates here once extended as far as the Markt. It was also the commercial and diplomatic centre for medieval Bruges, and foreign consulates opened along the length of Spiegelrei.

There is a statue of the painter in the square, but it is the buildings that really stand out. Jan looks directly at the most striking of these, the **Poortersloge** (Burghers' Lodge; 1417). The pencil tower may point heavenwards, but the building was in fact the meeting place of the wealthier city merchants. On its facade is a statue of the jolly bear that features in the city's coat of arms.

It was also the emblem of a jousting club that held its events in the marketplace outside. The restored building now houses the Bruges State Archives.

To the right of the Poortersloge is the 15th-century **Tolhuis** (Customs House), where various rulers levied tolls over the years, including the dukes of Luxembourg whose coat of arms is on the facade. This fine Gothic building now holds the library and documentation centre of West Flanders.

The Poortersloge

Adjacent Spanjaardstraat was the centre of the city's Spanish mercantile community in the 16th century and the many mansions in this area testify to their wealth. Among the best, at No. 16, is **Huis De la Torre** (*c.*1500), with an ornately decorated Gothic facade and a mid-16th-century Renaissance portal. Ignatius de Loyola, the Spanish priest who founded the Jesuit Order, was a frequent guest in the house at No. 9.

EAST OF JAN VAN EYCKPLEIN

From Jan van Eyckplein you can wander through the lovely canal-side street of Spinolarei into Koningstraat and Sint-Maartensplein, where you will find **Sint-Walburgakerk** (Church of St Walpurga). Pieter Huyssens, the Bruges Jesuit and architect, built this impressive Baroque church in 1643. A statue of St Francis Xavier stands above the entrance door. The Baroque interior is for the

Jeruzalemkapel

most part unremarkable, except for the fabulous pulpit by Artus Quellin the Younger, which has a scalloped canopy uplifted by trumpeting angels.

Crossing the canal and following Sint-Annarei south into Sint-Annakerkstraat, you will see the slender spire of **Sint-Annakerk** (Church of St Anne), a 1624 Baroque replacement for the Gothic church demolished in 1561. Inside, the carving of the rood screen, confessionals and pulpit, as well as the rich panelling, are well worth viewing if the church is open.

The unusual tower with the vaguely Oriental look visible from Sint-Annakerk belongs to the **Jeruzalemkapel** ⑮ (Jerusalem Chapel; www.adornes.org; Mon–Sat 10am–5pm), at Peperstraat 1. The church is modelled on the Church of the Holy Sepulchre in Jerusalem. Dating from 1428, it was built by the Adornes family, originally merchants from Genoa, who had travelled on a pilgrimage to Jerusalem. They were so impressed by the church that they built this one in Bruges. There is even a copy of Christ's memorial tomb in the crypt.

It is a sombre, stark place with good examples of 15th- and 16th-century stained glass, some of which depicts members of the Adornes family. In the nave you can see effigies of Anselmus Adornes and his wife. The altar is carved in a rather macabre fashion, with skulls and bones, and the cave-like atmosphere of the church is emphasised by the space behind the altar and above the crypt, which rises almost to the full height of the tower to create an eerie, artificial-looking cavern.

Beside Jeruzalemkerk is the **Kantcentrum** (Lace Centre; www.kantcentrum.eu; Mon–Sat 9.30am–5pm; see previous page), a museum and workshop in the 15th-century Jeruzalem-godshuizen (almshouses) founded by the Adornes family. Here you can see fine examples of the craft of lacemaking and demonstrations (Mon–Sat 2–5pm) by workers and their students.

A sign points down Balstraat towards the **Volkskundemuseum** (Folklore Museum; Tue–Sun 9.30am–5pm), at Balstraat 43, housed in a delightful row of 17th-century whitewashed almshouses built

⊙ LACEMAKING

Bruges' handmade lace is making a slow but steady comeback, thanks mainly to the demand from visiting tourists. At its peak in the 1840s, lacemaking provided steady employment – and low wages – for 10,000 local women and girls. Even in its heyday, lacemaking was a cottage industry. Handmade lace is expensive, and the majority of the items sold in the city's multitude of lace shops are machine-made and often imported.

The most popular kind of lace made in Bruges is bobbin lace, which is created using a technique developed in Flanders in the 16th century. Threads of silk, linen or cotton on as many as 700 different bobbins are crossed and braided around a framework of pins. It takes great skill and concentration to do this and it is fascinating to watch an experienced craftswoman (it generally is a woman) at work. Other styles of handmade Belgian lace are *bloemenwerk* (flower lace), *rozenkant* (pearled rosary) and *toveressesteek* (fairy stitch).

by the cobblers' guild. The life of everyday West Flanders is recreated in the traditionally furnished interiors, including a primary school class, coopers' and milliners' workshops, a sweet shop and everyday household scenes. A traditional alehouse, De Zwarte Kat (The Black Cat), offers respite for the weary walker.

Cross Rolweg into Carmersstraat and turn right to pass the **Engels Klooster Onze-Lieve-Vrouw van Nazareth** (English Convent of Our Lady of Nazareth) at No. 85, founded in 1629 by an order of English Ursuline nuns, with a domed church (1739). The last words of the Flemish poet-priest Guido Gezelle (see page 53), who died here in 1899, are carved on the facade: '...and I was so happy to hear the birds sing'.

Further up Carmersstraat, at 174, is the lodge of the **Schuttersgilde Sint-Sebastiaans** ⑯ (St Sebastian's Guild; www.sebastiaansgilde.be; Tue–Thu and Sat 2–5pm). The guild of archers was a powerful, wealthy and influential force in the city, and its sumptuous quarters (16th–17th centuries) reflect this. Inside are a collection of arms and accoutrements, furnishings, gold and silver plate, paintings and other works of art. Among the guild's past members are Belgian royalty, and England's King Charles II – who paid for the banqueting hall – and his brother Henry,

Lace is still made the traditional way at the Kantcentrum

both then in exile in Bruges. A portrait of Henry hangs above the fireplace.

Turn right into Kruisvest, where you will see, overlooking the canal, the **Sint-Janshuismolen** (St John's House Windmill; 1770; Tue–Sun 9.30am–12.30pm and 1.30–5pm). Turn right again into Rolweg, where at No. 64 stands the **Gezellemuseum** ⑰ (Tue–Sun 9.30am–12.30pm, 1.30–5pm), dedicated to the poet-priest Guido Gezelle (1830–99), in the house where he was born. Surrounded by a large garden, the brick-built, rather gloomy house contains objects related to Gezelle's life and work, including copies of manuscripts and editions of his poetry.

Return to Kruisvest and pass the **Bonne-Chièremolen**, a wooden stilt-windmill, then go right into Stijn Streuvelsstraat. At No. 59 is the lodge of the **Schuttersgilde Sint-Joris** (St George's Guild; tel: 050 33 54 08; www.st-jorisbrugge.be; open on request). Unlike the archers of St Sebastian's Guild, St George's members were crossbowmen. Their ornate guild house contains a fine collection of crossbows and the guild's archives. In the garden is a vertical target-mast and walkways protected from descending arrows.

WEST OF JAN VAN EYCKPLEIN

If you return to Jan van Eyckplein you can follow Acadamiestraat from the west side of the square. It joins Vlamingstraat, where at No. 35 you find the elegant **Huis Ter Beurze**. Now serving as a centre for conferences, receptions and exhibitions, the 15th-century house belonged to the Van der Beurze family. They leased rooms to city merchants, who lived and worked in the house; the family's name (rendered as 'bourse' or 'beurs') has come to designate the place for a commercial stock exchange in many languages.

The Genoese merchants in Bruges did their business in the adjacent building. Genuese Loge (Genoese Lodge), dating from 1441, now houses the **Frietmuseum** (Fries Museum; www.frietmuseum.be; daily 10am–5pm), dedicated to the humble but tasty – and somewhat misleadingly named – 'French' fries, or chips.

North of the Markt, there are no grand churches to compare with Onze-Lieve-Vrouwekerk or Sint-Salvatorskathedraal, but **Sint-Jakobskerk** ⑱ (St James's Church; summer daily 2–5pm; worshippers only during services) in Sint-Jakobsstraat makes the most determined bid for grandiosity. Thanks to generous gifts from the dukes of Burgundy, the 13th-century Gothic church was improved and enlarged to its present size. It has a pleasing internal harmony strangely lacking in many of the other churches in Bruges, and is illuminated by a pale pink light when the sun is shining. The interior is decorated with an abundance of 16th–18th-century paintings and tombs.

The glorious canopied pulpit is worth a closer inspection for its intricate, skilful carving. Among the most interesting of the tombs is the two-tiered arrangement of Ferry de Gros and his two wives. De Gros, who died in 1544, was a treasurer of the Order of the Golden Fleece. The tomb is reminiscent of the Italian Renaissance, with ornate floral designs on the ceramic wall-tiles. A walk of less than

Inside Onze-Lieve-Vrouw ter Potterie

1km (0.6 miles) along Ezelstraat leads past the 15th-century **Karmelietenkerk** (Carmelite Church) with its gloomy Baroque interior, to the **Ezelpoort** (Donkey Gate), or **Sint-Jacobspoort** (St James's Gate). One of the four surviving gates of the nine that once allowed passage through the 14th-century city walls, this formidable-looking bastion dates from 1370 and has been rebuilt several times.

NORTH OF JAN VAN EYCKPLEIN

Connected to Woensdagmarkt and Oosterlingenplein is Krom Genthof, a small square on which stands the **Oosterlingenhuis** (Easterners' House; 1481), once the local headquarters of the Hanseatic League, which was trading with Bruges as early as the 13th century. Part of the house survives in what is now the Hotel Bryghia.

For an insight into everyday Bruges, walk across the canal bridge into Potterierei, a different world from the busy city centre. Simply enjoy the peace and quiet, canalside houses, views and bridges. Near the far end of Potterierei a wooden gateway marks the entrance to the **Duinenabdij** (Abbey of the Dunes), a foundation that was based at Koksijde on the North Sea coast until it was forced to retreat from encroaching seas in 1560 and in the 17th century set up here. Since 1833 this has been the Episcopal Seminary.

Continue up Potterierei to No. 79, **Onze-Lieve-Vrouw ter Potterie ⓲** (Our Lady of the Pottery; museum Tue–Sun 9.30am–12.30pm, 1.30–5pm), formerly a hospice, with a recorded history going back to 1276. Most of the complex is now a senior citizens' home, but part of it – including a ward and cloisters dating from the 14th to the 15th centuries – has been opened as a museum. The collection includes tapestries, furniture from the 15th–17th centuries, silverware,

A paddle boat moored by Damme's windmill

religious objects and books, and early Flemish paintings. The adjoining 14th-century church, which used to be the Potters' Guild chapel, is a little gem, with a Baroque interior containing, among other treasures, a 13th-century statue of Our Lady of the Pottery said to have miraculous powers; and a 16th-century tapestry of the Nativity.

Return along Potterierei to the first bridge, a draw-bridge, cross over to Langerei, and keep going south. Turn right into Sint-Gilliskoorstraat, and then left along Lange Raamtstraat to the **Sint-Gilliskerk** (St Giles' Church), built around 1241 in the early Gothic style, but drastically altered in the 15th century, leaving it with three aisles in place of the earlier cruciform shape. Its treasures include a superb organ and a cycle of paintings from 1774 by Bruges artist Jan Garemijn, depicting the history of the Trinitarian Brothers. The artist Hans Memling was buried here in 1494.

EXCURSIONS

After the near perfection of Bruges, any other town in the region can seem disappointing, but there are several places of interest that you may like to explore on your way to or from the city. Most of them are no more than a few miles from Bruges. The exceptions are Ghent, the World War I battlefields around Ypres (Ieper), and Veurne. For descriptions of Brussels and Antwerp, see the *Berlitz Pocket Guide to Brussels*.

DAMME

The attractive roads leading to this picturesque village, 7km (4 miles) northeast of Bruges, are lined with pollarded trees, all kinked in exactly the same spot by the prevailing wind that blows across the open countryside. Once the outer port of its larger neighbour, **Damme 20** still retains an air of medieval prosperity, with some fine old buildings and excellent restaurants around its marketplace. With a windmill, and skating on the canal in winter, Damme is a picture-postcard Flemish village.

Damme's main street (Kerkstraat) has a delightful **Stadhuis** (Town Hall) built in 1468, with four corner turrets. In front of the building stands a statue of the poet Jacob van Maerlant (1230–96), who wrote his most important works in Damme. The white sandstone facade is adorned with further statues of historic notables including Charles the Bold and Margaret of York. At one corner, two 'stones of

---

Bruges to Damme

In the summer, you can take a paddleboat canal cruise from Noorwegse Kaai in Bruges to Damme. Alternatively, take a No. 4 bus from the railway station – or walk or cycle along the canalside paths.

The eye-catching Stadhuis in Damme

justice' hang from the wall. They used to be tied to the neck or feet of unfortunate women who had given offence in some way, who were then made to parade round the village.

To the right of the building is **De Grote Sterre** (The Great Star), a twin-gabled 15th-century house that was the home of the Spanish governor in the 17th century. Almost destroyed in a storm in 1990, it has undergone extensive restoration. It now houses the tourist information office. Four doors further down is the 15th-century house where the wedding party of Charles the Bold and Margaret of York was held in 1468. Royal weddings were celebrated in lavish style: the festivities in Bruges lasted for two weeks.

Sint-Janshospitaal (St John's Hospital) is across the road and down from the Stadhuis. Founded in 1249, it includes a Baroque chapel and a museum of paintings, liturgical objects and sacred books. Further up the street and visible from the museum is the 13th-century tower of one of Bruges' prominent beacons, the **Onze-Lieve-Vrouwekerk** (Church of Our Lady). The church has endured many alterations down the centuries, including a fire started in 1578 by soldiers of William of Orange. The tower, gaining its present appearance as a result of partial demolition in 1725, is now the haunt of jackdaws. The separate nave, which has been restored, can be visited in the summer, when the site seems less menacing.

Signposts lead you to the town's former herring market, which comprises an attractive circle of whitewashed cottages surrounding the village's first drinking-water pump.

DUDZELE

Just north of Bruges, this village beside the Boudewijn Kanaal to Zeebrugge, lies on the route to Lissewege. Pause for a look at the ruined 12th-century Romanesque **tower** at **Sint-Pieters-Bandenkerk** (Church of St Peter in Chains) in the centre. Across the road is a small museum of local history, the **Heemkundigmuseum De Groene Tente** (The Green Tent; www.degroenetente.be; currently closed for renovation until further notice).

LISSEWEGE

This pretty village of whitewashed old houses north of Bruges stands along the **Lisseweegs Vaartje**, a narrow canal that in medieval times connected Lissewege and Bruges. In the main square, Onder de Toren, stands the early Gothic **Onze-Lieve-Vrouw-Bezoekingskerk** (Church of Our Lady of the Visitation), dating from 1225–50, with a flat-topped tower 50m (162ft) high, from which a carillon tune occasionally bursts forth. Inside the church are a superb Baroque organ, 17th- and 18th-century paintings, and a replica of a statue of the Madonna and Child

Riding on the sands at De Haan

– said to have been miraculous – destroyed by Dutch Protestants in the 16th century.

ZEEBRUGGE

A visit to the port and coastal resort of **Zeebrugge** ㉑ ('Sea Bruges') should add to your understanding of the main city. The harbour theme park, **Seafront Zeebrugge** (www.seafront.be; daily 10am–5pm), is full of interest, especially for children. Among its many maritime attractions are the old West-Hinder lightship; an interactive exhibition on life on, below and beside the sea; and boat tours of the harbour.

DE HAAN

Widely considered the jewel of the Belgian coast, **De Haan** ㉒ (Le Coq in French) is 16km (10 miles) from Bruges. The central area of De Haan, known as De Concessie (The Concession), is filled with Belle Epoque villas, some converted to hotels and some privately owned. De Haan's tourist office is housed in the 1902 **Tramstation** at Koninklijk Plein, which has Art Nouveau lines and later Art Deco features. Close by are two pagoda-like pavilions, now kiosks, built in 1904 for the town's Casino, which was itself built in 1899 and has since been demolished. The **Hotel Des Brasseurs** is another Belle Epoque gem with Art Nouveau elements. Facing it is the domed **Grand Hotel Belle Vue**, opened in the 1920s in what was a private villa. In adjacent Rembrandtlaan a cluster of villas dating from 1925–7 are listed as historic monuments.

From Koninklijk Plein, walk north along Leopoldlaan past the **Hotel Heritage**, the Art Deco **Hotel Astoria** (1930) and the striking **Stadhuis** (Town Hall; 1899), originally the Grand Hôtel du Coq-sur-Mer. After fleeing from Nazi Germany, in 1933 Albert Einstein lived for six months in the **Villa Savoyarde**, in Jean d'Ardennelaan, west of the Town Hall. Parallel to Leopoldlaan is Maria Hendrikalaan; at No. 20 is the Zee-Linde vacation centre (once known as **Hotel Atlanta**), formerly Crown Prince Albert's villa (1901).

With its safe waters and golden sands, De Haan is a popular family resort. Part of the beach, which is lined with open-air café

⊙ THE COAST TRAM

Belgium's North Sea coastline stretches 64km (40 miles) from the Dutch to the French border. Access to the entire coast is made easy by the *Kusttram* (Coast Tram), which in two hours runs almost the full length of the shore, between Knokke-Heist and De Panne. It is the world's longest tramline, with 67km (42 miles) of tracks. These pass through chic Knokke-Heist, the busy port of Zeebrugge, the yacht harbour at Blankenberge, Belle Epoque De Haan, bustling Ostend, the fishing harbour of Nieuwpoort and the long beaches of Oostduinkerke and De Panne. For a considerable part of the way the tram runs along just behind the sand dunes; on other stretches it plunges into busy towns like Ostend and Zeebrugge. You can use it either as a touring option or as a straightforward, fast way to get from one place to another. The *Kusttram* is operated by the public transport company of Flanders, De Lijn (tel: 059-56 52 11; www.delijn.be/dekusttram).

terraces, is designated for windsurfing. Just west of the resort, golfers play the 18-hole links course of the **Koninklijke Golf Club Oostende** (Royal Ostend Golf Club; www.golfoostende.be), bordered by the **Natuurreservaat De Kijkuit** (De Kijkuit Nature Reserve; www.natuurpunt.be) and its protected sand dunes.

OOSTENDE (OSTEND)

The 'Queen of the Coast', Belgium's liveliest North Sea resort, is quickly reached by train from Bruges. Outside **Oostende ㉓** railway station stands a reminder of the town's maritime heritage. The green-hulled **Amandine** (www.zeilschipmercator.be; daily 10am–5pm), built in 1961, ended her Arctic voyaging in 1995. This last of Ostend's Iceland-bound trawlers is now permanently 'moored' at the edge of the harbour, in a dry basin. Adjacent **Visserskaai** (Fishermen's Wharf) is lined with seafood restaurants and seafood stalls. On the harbour side, you can see fish, shellfish and sea plants in the **Noordzeeaquarium** (North Sea Aquarium; Apr–June, Sept–Dec Mon–Fri 10.30am–12.30pm, 1–5pm, Sat–Sun 10.30am–1pm, 1.30–5.30pm; July–Aug weekdays 10am–5.30pm). Close by is the **Vistrap** (Fish Market), where the day's trawler catch is sold.

Post-war apartments line Albert I Promenade, replacing demolished 19th-century mansions on the once-fashionable seafront esplanade. Turn left into Vlaanderenstraat, to the 19th-century **Ensorhuis** (Wed–Mon 10am–noon, 2–5pm), at No. 27, where the Anglo-Belgian painter James Ensor lived from 1916 until his death in 1949. In Ensor's time, this undistinguished town house had a souvenir shop on the ground floor and his studio on the first. Continuing beside the beach brings you to the **Casino-Kursaal** (www.kursaaloostende.be), a 1950s replacement for an 1887 original blown up by the Germans in World War II. In addition to gaming tables, there are restaurants and cafés.

You now reach the 19th-century **Venetiaanse Gaanderijen** (Venetian Galleries). At the entrance to this former royal pavilion is a bronze sculpture of King Baudouin (1951–93), on foot and wearing a raincoat, on a visit to Ostend. Albert I Promenade joins the Zeedijk (Sea Dike) as you come face to face with an equestrian statue (dating from 1931) of King Leopold II (1865–1909). Adjacent to this begins the long **Koninklijke**

Casino-Kursaal at Oostende

Gaanderijen (Royal Galleries), built in 1906 by French architect Charles Girault so that Leopold II and his court could shelter from the wind as they passed along the seafront. The plush Art Deco Thermae Palace hotel in the middle dates from 1933.

Head east on Koningin Astridlaan and Warschauwstraat to Leopold I Plein, with its **equestrian statue** of King Leopold I (1831–65). If you are interested in modern art, you could make a long trek south on Rogierlaan, then into Romestraat to the **Kunst Museum aan Zee** (Art Museum by the Sea; www.muzee. be; Tue–Sun 10am–6pm) at No. 11. In this converted Modernist department store you can see mostly Belgian works by the likes of Panamarenko and Jan Fabre. Take Witte Nonnenstraat to Wapenplein, a square with a wrought-iron bandstand in the middle. Across the square, at Langestraat 69, is the **Stadsmuseum Oostende** (www.oostende.be; Wed–Mon 10am–12.30pm, 2–6pm), which retells the city's maritime history.

At the end of Kerkstraat is the colossal neo-Gothic edifice **of Sint-Petrus-en-Pauluskerk** (Church of Sts Peter and Paul). Inside is the tomb of Belgium's first queen, Marie-Louise of Orléans, who died in Ostend in 1850. Back at the harbour, in Vindictivelaan, the yacht harbour hosts the elegant, three-masted schooner **Mercator** (daily 10am–5pm), a merchant marine training ship that spends most of its time here as a floating museum.

VEURNE

Just 6km (4 miles) from the border with France is the small town of **Veurne** ㉔, with a population not much greater than that of Damme. Veurne grew from a 9th-century fortress and now has an attractive central marketplace, among the best in Belgium. The town's *Boetprocessie* (Procession of the Penitents) takes place on the last Sunday in July, presenting scenes from Christ's Passion. Owing much to Spanish influence (the town once served as a Spanish garrison), the procession is similar to the Spanish celebration of *Semana Santa* (Holy Week). Other processions are staged during Easter and Lent.

Most of Veurne's places of interest are in or alongside the central Grote

Sint-Walburgakerk, Veurne

Markt, where you will also find plenty of cafés and restaurants. In the summer months, tickets for guided tours and carriage rides through the town are available from the tourist office in the square.

The typical yellow Flemish brick is much in evidence, together with an architectural style that shows a restrained Spanish influence. The gabled **Stadhuis** (Town Hall) in the Grote Markt, built in 1612, has an attractive loggia of bluestone contrasting with the yellow brick of the rest of the structure. Visitors can join guided tours of the interior, which features some unusual and impressive leather wall hangings originating from Córdoba in southern Spain.

The **Landhuis**, adjoining the Stadhuis, was built in 1616, its Gothic bell-tower topped with a Baroque spire. It houses the tourist information office. Next door is a delightful parade of five houses with step gables, each with a different design of columns around the windows. The cafés on the ground floors spill out into the square on warm days. On the northeast side of the square is the **Spaans Paviljoen** (Spanish Pavilion), which as the name suggests, was the headquarters for Spanish officers during the 17th century. Across the road, the building with all the window shutters is the Renaissance **Vleeshuis** (Meat Market), built in 1615, and now a library.

The imposing, unfinished tower of **Sint-Niklaaskerk** (Church of St Nicholas), rising from nearby Appelmarkt, can be climbed to get a good view; the 13th-century structure has a carillon. The other church in the town is **Sint-Walburgakerk** (Church of St Walpurga), construction of which began in 1250 with ambitious plans that eventually proved too much for the little town. It has a splendid 27m (90ft) nave. The interior of the church is worth a visit, more for its overall effect than for any specific item, though there is a fine Baroque pulpit.

YPRES AND FLANDERS FIELDS

Southwest of Bruges towards the border with France lies **Flanders Fields**, a vast area of countryside that witnessed military carnage on an unprecedented scale. Although the senseless waste of millions of lives in World War I has gone down in history, the staggering numbers killed nevertheless still have the power to shock. Row upon row of gravestones in the many cemeteries of the area testify to the butchery of war. Whether or not you have relatives buried here, the peacefulness of the place and the solidarity in death of troops from all sides make for a moving and strangely comforting experience – the soldiers' ordeal is at an end.

Ypres ㉕ (Ieper) is a name that still resonates in collective memory. The focus of repeated attacks and counter-attacks, it was shelled to destruction during World War I, then carefully reconstructed over the next 40 years. Nothing old remains in the bustling town, but it has an open, relaxed central Grote Markt and an imposing Stadhuis. The **In Flanders Fields Museum** (www.inflandersfields.be; Apr–mid-Nov daily 10am–6pm; mid-Nov–Mar Tue–Sun 10am–5pm) is a striking

⊙ TOURS OF REMEMBRANCE

There are coach tours available from Bruges that visit selected towns, war cemeteries and memorials. Alternatively, if you wish to take more time and follow your own inclinations, it is worth taking a car (or even a bicycle) and making use of 'Route 14–18', a sign-posted route through the battlefield area of the Ypres Salient. It should be stressed, however, that nothing much remains of the battlefields. Where you wish to go will depend on any family connections you may have with the war, and our survey of sites is necessarily selective.

Information plaque about the Last Post ceremony

interactive museum located in the reconstructed **Lakenhalle** (Cloth Hall). It uses historical documents, film footage, poetry, song and sound effects to evoke the brutal experience of trench warfare in the Ypres Salient.

The **Menin Gate** memorial, located just off the Grote Markt, is built on a cutting through which thousands of men made their way towards the Ypres Salient. Designed by Reginald Blomfield, it comprises a classical facade fronting a vast arch with three open ceiling oculi. It is inscribed with the names of nearly 55,000 British soldiers who died in battle but have no known graves.

Every evening at 8pm, the Last Post is played here by local volunteer buglers to commemorate those who died. This ceremony has taken place every evening since July 1928, except for the period when the city was occupied by the German army during World War II.

THE WAR CEMETERIES

On Hill 62, just southeast of Ypres near Zillebeke, stands a memorial to the Canadian troops who lost their lives. Near the hill, **Sanctuary Wood Cemetery** preserves a few remaining sections of trench. At Hill 60, a little further beyond Zillebeke, a roadside memorial commemorates the fallen of Australia, behind which lies a field of mounds and hollows, created by intensive bombardment, where you can still make out the ruins of bunkers. This 'strategically important' hill was constantly taken and retaken throughout World War I. Today, sheep graze here and birds sing in the trees.

A little over 10km (6 miles) northeast of Ypres, situated off the N332 before Passendale (Passchendaele), is **Tyne Cot Commonwealth War Graves Cemetery ㉖**. Designed by the architect Sir Herbert Baker, the cemetery was intended to evoke the appearance of a traditional English graveyard, with white gravestones standing honourably in regular formation on a neat green lawn. Its large Cross of Sacrifice in Portland stone is built on the site of the Tyne Cot dressing station that was finally captured by Australian troops in 1917. The slight rise on which the cemetery is located affords a view over the now peaceful countryside.

The German cemetery located at **Langemark**, approximately 16km (10 miles) north of Ypres, contains the remains of more than 44,000 German soldiers – over half of them in a mass grave. It is referred to as the Students' Cemetery because so many young soldiers perished in the Ypres Salient in 1914 and 1915. The gravestones are simple tablets that lie flush with the lawn, on ground sheltered by mature trees. The cemetery contains the remnants of three bunkers.

Further northwest, 4km (2.5 miles) outside the town of Diksmuide, **Vladslo** German cemetery is the site of more than 25,000 German graves and an extremely moving memorial sculpture by Käthe Kollwitz (1867–1945) entitled *Grieving Parents*. The German sculptor's younger son, Peter, killed in October 1914, lies buried there.

In fact, there are more than 150 war cemeteries in this area, making it seem as if Flanders Fields belong more to the dead than to the living.

Tyne Cot is the largest military cemetery in the world

SINT-ANDRIES

Two large country estates are embedded in the forests a short distance southwest of Bruges, in the city's **Sint-Andries** ㉗ suburb. **Domein Beisbroek** has a **Natuurcentrum** (Nature Centre; Wed 2.30–6pm, Fri 8–10pm, Sun 2.30–6pm; free), a **Volkssterrenwacht** (Observatory; www.cozmix.be; open for pre-arranged groups) and the **Zeiss Planetarium** (displays Wed and Sun 3pm and 4.30pm, Fri 8.30pm), which explains the mysteries of the night sky.

At nearby **Domein Tudor** the splendid neo-Gothic **Kasteel Tudor** (Tudor Castle; www.feestzaalzoeker.be/kasteel-tudor), built in 1904, is run as a celebrations room and seminar centre.

TILLEGEMBOS

Take bus No. 25, alight at 'Vozelzang' stop, and walk 900m along Kervyndreef to the woods of **Tillegembos** ㉘ in Bruges' south-western suburb, Sint-Michiels. They cover an area of 80 hectares (200 acres), providing a rural retreat from the city. Lots of well-marked footpaths lead you around this former estate, and there is also a lakeside inn, a picturesque mill and play areas for children. The on-site moated **Kasteel Tillegem**, a fortress dating from the 14th century, is the headquarters of the West Flanders Province and only open during heritage days (ask tourist board).

KASTEEL LOPPEM

Situated just 3km (2 miles) south of Bruges is the neo-Gothic **Kasteel Loppem** ㉙ (www.kasteelvanloppem.be; Mar–Nov Tue–Sat 2–6pm). It was conceived by August Pugin, architect of the British Houses of Parliament, and later completed by Jean Béthune. Built between 1858 and 1863, the house is sumptuously decorated; the tone dominated by the wood of the ceilings and furniture, as well as numerous artworks. It has a private chapel and a wonderful, soaring hall, and the extensive gardens feature a 19th-century hedge labyrinth (opening hours vary, see website for details) for children to explore.

⊙ WHO PAINTED THE ALTERPIECE?

Whether or not van Eyck really was responsible for *The Adoration of the Mystic Lamb* has in the past been a matter of some dispute. An inscription on the frame of the altarpiece declares that it was started by his brother Hubert van Eyck and completed by Jan. However, since no-one has any other evidence for the existence of Hubert, it is thought by many that he was the mythical creation of Ghent citizens jealous of Bruges' monopolising of Jan. Certainly, it is difficult to believe that an artist of van Eyck's genius could be surpassed by someone who has otherwise left nothing to posterity. Most art historians today unhesitatingly attribute the work of this painting solely to the master artist Jan van Eyck.

GHENT

Ghent (Gent in Dutch),
lies at the confluence of
the rivers Scheldt and Leie.
The city is a little larger
than Bruges, but most of
its historic attractions are
clustered together within
walking distance of one
another. It is a city built on
diverse economic interests,
with the sense to preserve
its historical heart. That
past is shown in some magnificent buildings spread

Houses along Ghent's Korenlei

along canals, second only to those of Bruges in splendour. Quaint
trams trundle through the cobbled centre of this inland port city,
which has an almost Mediterranean air about it thanks to the
tables of cafés and bars spilling out onto the pavements.

Our tour starts from Sint-Baafsplein. Most of Ghent's historic
Inner Town lies northwest of this square, straddling the Y-shaped
meeting of the two rivers. This area is one of winding streets and
alleyways, while the south is lined with elegant boulevards and
imposing mansions.

SINT-BAAFSKATHEDRAAL

The largely Gothic brick and granite **Sint-Baafskathedraal**
A (St Bavo's Cathedral; www.sintbaafskathedraal.be; Apr–
Oct Mon–Sat 8.30am–6pm, Sun 1–6pm, Nov–Mar Mon–Sat
8.30am–5pm, Sun 1–5pm) was constructed over the course of
several centuries. The chancel dates from the turn of the 14th

century, both the tower and the nave from the 15th century, and the transept from the mid-16th century. In the nave, a forest of stone leads the eye upwards to a glorious late-Gothic display of rib vaulting in the roof. The tower (currently being renovated) contains a carillon, and the crypt retains some of the structure of an earlier Romanesque church.

The cathedral's greatest treasure is located in a side chapel to the left of the main entrance, variously known as the *Ghent Altarpiece* or *The Adoration of the Mystic Lamb* (Mon–Fri 10.30am–4pm, until 5pm in summer, Sun 1–5pm). This marvellous panel painting is regarded as the crowning achievement of Jan van Eyck's Gothic style, which broke completely with medieval ideas and styles and instituted a new kind of realism.

The altarpiece seems to become increasingly detailed the closer you look at it, and the painting is invested with humanity and optimism, with God the Father looking kindly upon it all. If you look carefully, you will see Bruges Cathedral in the background of the central panel.

There are many other important works of art in the cathedral. Rubens' painting of 1624, *The Conversion of St Bavo*, is full of the unique drama with which the artist infused all his work. Also of interest is Frans Pourbus the Elder's *Christ Among the Doctors*, painted in 1571. A youthful Jesus is shown amazing the elders of the temple with his knowledge and wisdom, but it is his audience that claims our attention: Pourbus portrayed contemporary luminaries such as Philip II and Charles V, Thomas Calvin, and even his rival, painter

Tourist office

Ghent's tourist office is based inside the renovated Oude Vismijn (Old Fish Market) on Sint-Veerleplein. It is open daily Apr–Sept 9.30am–6.30pm, Oct–Mar 9.30am–4.30pm.

Pieter Brueghel the Elder in the crowd. Down in the crypt is the striking *Calvary Triptych* of Justus van Gent, painted in 1466.

You will also find splendid examples of sculpture, the best of which is the Baroque oak and marble pulpit, one of Laurent Delvaux's masterpieces, completed in 1741. The dynamic, intricate carving of the design sweeps the eye up to where the preacher would stand,

The towering Belfry

above which a marble tree of knowledge grows complete with gilded serpent and fruit. St Bavo himself is commemorated in the Baroque high altar of sculptor Hendrik Frans Verbruggen.

THE BELFORT AND LAKENHALLE

Opposite the cathedral, the **Belfort** Ⓑ (Belfry; daily 10am–6pm), completed in 1380, has since become the pre-eminent symbol of the city's independence and houses one of the best carillons in Belgium. You can view the 53 bells on the fifth floor using the glass lift and ascend to the top of the 91m (298ft) tower for spectacular views across the city.

The gilded copper dragon at the top of the spire was first installed upon completion of the tower, but the creature and the four figures now poised at the corners of the viewing platform are modern replicas. The spire itself was restored at the beginning of the 20th century according to the original 14th-century design.

In front, stands the ultra-modern steel-and-wood Stadshal – a meeting place and site of the Belfort Stadscafé and restaurant (see page 108).

The neighbouring **Lakenhalle** (Cloth Hall) is another display of Ghent's civic pride and bygone wealth. The building, much restored, dates from 1441, once serving as the meeting place for the city's wool and cloth traders.

BOTERMARKT AND HOOGPOORT

Across the road from the Lakenhalle in Botermarkt stands the formidable **Stadhuis** Ⓒ (Town Hall; guided visits only). All pilasters and windows, the Stadhuis is like a catalogue of architecture: the oldest part of the building (on the Hoogpoort side) dates from the early 16th century and, with its florid design and ornate statues, follows the style of Bruges' Stadhuis. Religious disputes in 1539 and the economic decline of Ghent halted the work for some 60 years. Work began again with the Renaissance-style facade of the Botermarkt side of the hall; it was continued in the 18th century with the Baroque facade facing the corner of Hoogpoort and Stadhuissteeg and the rococo Poeljemarkt side. The throne room and an impressive city council room are accessible to visitors. It is worth joining their guided tours. Don't miss the City Pavilion on Poeljemarkt, a modern counterpoint to the nearby historical buildings. This multifunctional architectural gem is made of glass, wood and concrete and hosts concerts, dance performances and markets. It makes for an excellent meeting point or

Canal cruises

Like Bruges, Ghent offers canal boat cruises in summer. It is also fun to tour the city by tram: the main tram terminus is outside Sint-Pieters train station.

Cruising along Korenlei

refreshment stop: the semi-underground spacious Belfort Stadscafé has a nice terrace and great views.

North from St Baafsplein, Hoogpoort runs northwest past some beautiful Ghent houses. On the corner with the square stands **Sint-Jorishof**, the former house of the Guild of Crossbowmen (now a hotel), built in 1477. It was here that Mary of Burgundy granted a charter of freedoms to the Flemish cloth towns. Hoogpoort leads to Groentenmarkt, site of the medieval pillory and former vegetable market. The **Groot Vleeshuis**, on the west side of the square, comprises a complex of gabled buildings restored in 1912 but dating from 1406. The buildings include a covered meat market, a guild house and a chapel.

Korenmarkt (Corn Market) connects via Kortemunt with Groentenmarkt; at its southern end stands the landmark **Sint-Niklaaskerk ①** (St Nicholas' Church), from where Sint-Michielsbrug (St Michael's Bridge) spans the Leie River. The

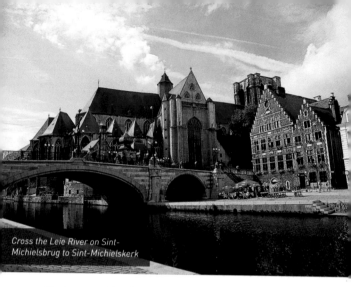

Cross the Leie River on Sint-Michielsbrug to Sint-Michielskerk

oldest parts of the Gothic Sint-Niklaaskerk date back to the 13th century, but the building was not completed until five centuries later. Inside, the Baroque high altar is a typically energetic design of the period. The whole church is flooded with a beautiful light on sunny days. This area offers some of the most characteristic views of Ghent; you can make out the towers of the Belfry and Sint-Baaf's Cathedral, the picturesque Korenlei and Graslei quaysides, and the ominous mass of Gravensteen, the Castle of the Counts. Across from the bridge you will see **Sint-Michielskerk** (St Michael's Church), which acts as a kind of visual counterbalance to Sint-Niklaaskerk.

KORENLEI AND GRASLEI

North from Sint-Michielsbrug, you can stroll on both banks of the river, past a splendid array of medieval guild houses on the quaysides. **Korenlei**, on the left, and **Graslei**, on the right, comprise Ghent's oldest harbour, the **Tussen Bruggen** (Between the Bridges). This area was the commercial heart of the medieval city and the place where Ghent's wealthy guilds chose to build.

Along Korenlei, a building to watch out for is the **Gildehuis van de Onvrije Schippers** (House of the Tied Boatmen), at No. 7, built in 1739, an excellent example of Flemish Baroque, with spectacular dolphins and lions adorning the gables and a gilded ship crowning the roof. Another is the 16th-century **De Zwane** (The Swan) at No. 9, a former brewery that has a graceful swan depicted in two carvings on the gables.

Look over the water to Graslei for a view of the even finer houses on that quay before crossing for a closer inspection. The **Gildehuis van de Vrije Schippers** (House of the Free Boatmen) was built in 1531, in Brabant Gothic style, while next door, the second Baroque **Gildehuis van de Graanmeters** (House of the Grain Weighers) dates back to 1698.

The little **Tolhuisje** (Customs House), built in 1682 in a narrow alley, looks like an attractive Renaissance afterthought. Next door is the Romanesque-style **Het Spijker**, also known as Koornstapelhuis (a former grain warehouse), dating from about 1200, and on the other side is the **Korenmetershuis** (Corn Measurer's house), followed by the Gothic **Gildehuis van de Metselaars** (House of the Masons), dating from 1527 and built in Brabant Gothic style.

NORTH OF KORENLEI

Jan Breydelstraat branches off from the north end of Korenlei. At No. 5, occupying a house built in 1755 by

CityCard Ghent

Valid for 48 or 72 hours, the CityCard Ghent grants free entry to all Ghent's historic sites and museums. It costs €30/35 and can be bought at the tourist information office.

the De Coninck family, is the **Design Museum Gent ❺** (Thu–Tue 10am–5.30pm). It is devoted to interior design and furnishings in rooms decorated mainly in 18th-century style. There is also a wonderful Art Nouveau collection, the best in the country, and some fine examples of Art Deco, as well as more modern pieces.

Further along, in adjacent Burgstraat, the Renaissance-gabled house decorated with portraits of the Counts of Flanders is the **Huis der Gekroonde Hoofden** (House of the Crowned Heads), now housing a restaurant of the same name.

GRAVENSTEEN

Turning right onto St Veerleplein leads to the heavily reno-vated island fortress called the **Gravensteen ❻** (Castle of the Counts; https://gravensteen.stad.gent/en; daily Apr–Oct 10am–6pm, Nov–Mar 9am–5pm). The castle is still a powerful and ominous presence here, with massive fortifications com-prising crenelated cylindrical towers and a vast brooding keep.

Work began on the structure in 1180 on the site of a 9th-century castle, on the orders of Philip of Alsace. The building was closely modelled on the Crusader castles of the Holy Land; a climb along the battlements (particularly at the top of the keep) provides excellent views and a welcome blast of fresh air. A tunnel leads to the central courtyard, which is surrounded by turreted walls, and the central keep may be reached via a spiral staircase. Inside, the keep contains the living quarters of a succession of Counts of Flanders, including the impressive Great Hall where Philip the Good fêted the Knights of the Golden Fleece in 1445.

FROM KRAANLEI TO VRIJDAGMARKT

Kraanlei is lined with fine houses; at No. 65 the almshouses are now home to **Huis van Alijn** (Alijn House; www.huisvanalijn.be; Mon–Tue, Thu–Fri 9am–5pm, Sat–Sun 10am–6pm), the city's folklore museum. Built in 1363, this beautifully restored complex is comprised of 18 interconnected cottages arranged around a courtyard. Each room is decorated in typical 1900 style. The everyday life of working people is evoked through the items and tools they would have known and used and the few luxuries they could afford.

View over Ghent's centre and cathedral

Crossing the Leie via the Zuivelbrug leads to Grootkannonplein, where you will meet **Dulle Griet** (Mad Meg); a 16-tonne cannon made in the 15th century, standing on the quayside, supported by three stone plinths.

Just a few steps away, **Vrijdagmarkt** (Friday Market) has some excellent examples of guild houses, with a 19th-century monument to Ghent hero Jacob van Artevelde at the centre of the square. The stylish Art Nouveau building named **Ons Huis**, which was built in 1900, used to belong to the Socialist Workers' Association; it is attractive in itself, though it appears too tall for the square. Older houses include Nos 22 and 43–7, built in the 17th and 18th centuries respectively.

In this square the Flemish Counts were sworn in by the citizens of the city. Visible from the square at Koningstraat 18, the **Koninklijke Vlaamse Academie voor Taal** (Royal Flemish Academy for Languages) is an imposing Baroque mansion that looms over the entire length of the street. A short walk north-east from here, on Minnemeers 10, is the excellent interactive Museum of Industry, Work and Textile (MIAT; tel: 09 269 42 00; www.miat.gent.be; Mon–Tue, Thu–Fri 9am–5pm, weekends and holidays 10am–6pm). Housed in an old cotton mill by the River Leie, the museum is spread over five floors, and documents technological manufacturing changes of the last 250 years. Exhibitions include old textile machinery as well as an interesting, if slightly sobering, section on child labour. The museum also boasts beautiful views across the city from upper floors.

AROUND VELDSTRAAT

Veldstraat, running south from Sint-Niklaaskerk, is the city's main shopping street, as you will soon realise from the crowds (the street is pedestrianised, but watch out for trams). Many of the original building exteriors remain. The most flamboyant of these, at no.55, is the **Hotel d'Hane-Steenhuyse** (Fri–Sat 2.30–5pm). The eye-catching rococo facade of this 18th-century mansion is matched only by the classical facade of its garden frontage. Louis XVIII lived here briefly when he fled from Napoleon; other inhabitants have included the French writer and statesman Talleyrand and members of the Russian royal family.

At No. 82, the **Museum Arnold Vander Haeghen** (Fri–Sat 8am-noon, 2–4pm) is devoted to the library of Nobel Prize-winning writer Maurice Maeterlinck (1862–1949) and Ghent graphic artist Victor Stuyvaert. The house was built in 1741; in 1815 it was home to the Duke of Wellington. It has a charming Chinese salon with silk wallpaper and some 18th- and 19th-century interior designs; it also hosts a variety of temporary exhibitions.

Turn left at Zonnestraat to **Kouter** and you will find yourself in a large square that has good claim to being the most historically significant one in the city. A variety of festivals, military parades, political demonstrations, meetings, archery contests and tournaments have taken place here through the centuries, and a flower market has been held in the square on Sunday since the 18th century. It may be difficult to envisage all the pomp of the past, as very few buildings of any antiquity have survived; exceptions to this are the house at No. 29 and the Opera House, situated off the square in Schouwburgstraat, and completed in 1840.

FINE ARTS MUSEUMS

A 10-minute walk along Charles de Kerchovelaan leads to **Citadelpark**. In the eastern corner of the park is the **Museum voor Schone Kunsten ⑥** (Museum of Fine Arts; www.mskgent. be; Tue–Sun 10am–5.30pm). The strange art of Hieronymus Bosch is represented by *Christ Carrying the Cross*, an unforgettable painting showing Christ on the way to Calvary.

Among other Flemish and Dutch exhibits are works by Jacob Jordaens, Frans Hals' bravura *Old Lady* – full of exuberant brushwork – Pieter Brueghel the Younger's *Peasant Wedding* and a rather harassed *Village Advocate*. Rubens is represented by a *Scourging of Christ* and *St Francis Receiving the Stigmata*. Later paintings include works by Géricault, Corot, Courbet, Daumier, Ensor and Rouault. The former casino opposite the Museum of Fine Arts is now occupied by **SMAK** (Museum of Contemporary

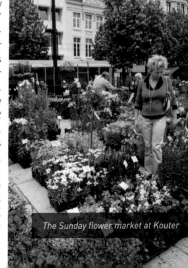

The Sunday flower market at Kouter

⊙ HOW FLANDERS INFLUENCED ART

Medieval Flanders bequeathed some of the most profound and best-loved paintings to the world, the greatest of which can be seen in Bruges and Ghent. The brilliance of painters such as Bosch, Memling and van Eyck sprang from the Gothic tradition that nurtured them. Gothic art was essentially a religious art form, with devotional paintings depicting the life of Christ, the Virgin Mary and the saints, but in Flanders it also came to place great emphasis on the accurate representation of the world, which was seen as God's creation and a vehicle for the sacred.

Van Eyck retained the religious subject matter of the Gothic tradition, but used the revolutionary medium of oil, enabling greater control. No artist before him had observed nature so minutely, or was capable of rendering observations so precisely. His paintings, along with those of Memling and artists such as Petrus Christus, Hugo van der Goes and Pieter Pourbus, reinforce this truthfulness to appearance.

The combination of sacred theme and faithful depiction of the world was taken a stage further a hundred years after van Eyck in the work of Brueghel the Elder, whose paintings of biblical events are set in the recognisable peasant world of his time.

Nevertheless, the genius of an artist usually needs fertile soil in which to grow. For a long time the wealth of the Burgundian court and the merchant class of Bruges and Ghent was enough to pay for the commissioning of new works.

Eventually the economic centre of gravity moved northward to Antwerp (home to Rubens and his pupil Van Dyck) and the Netherlands, where the first sophisticated market for genre paintings developed. Inevitably, the influence of Flemish painting moved with the money.

Art; www.smak.be; Tue–Sun 10am–5.30pm). The permanent collection is mainly devoted to Belgian and international artists since 1945, with works by Bacon, Panamarenko, Broodthaers, Long and Nauman. The museum also has a reputation for outstanding temporary exhibitions.

Just north of the Leie canal, at Godshuizenlaan 2, is **STAM** (Stadmuseum Gent; www.stamgent.be; Thu–Tue 10am–5.30pm), a dynamic museum outlining the city's history.

The Baroque dome of Sint-Pieterskerk

SINT-PIETERSPLEIN

North of the museum, Overpoortstraat leads to Sint-Pieters-plein, where there are regular exhibitions of art and other cultural events at the **Kunsthal Sint-Pietersabdij** (St Peter's Abbey Arts Centre; Tue–Sun 10am–6pm).

The splendid 57m (188ft) cupola of **Onze-Lieve-Vrouw Sint-Pieterskerk** 🅗 (Church of Our Lady of St Peter) can be seen for many streets around. The Baroque church was designed by the Huyssens brothers and built in 1719. Clearly, the architects were not lacking in ambition: the design is based on St Peter's Basilica in Rome. The impressive facade dominates attractive Sint-Pietersplein; the church has an exuberant Baroque-style interior and artworks by Van Dyck. From Sint-Pietersplein, Sint-Kwintensberg leads to Nederkouter, and then Veldstraat.

Take a ride around Bruges
in a horse-drawn carriage

WHAT TO DO

SHOPPING

The thought of shopping in Bruges may not immediately leap to mind, but the city has a large range of stores of all descriptions. Bruges is adapted to the lucrative tourist trade so you will find plenty of specialised stores and souvenirs. Except for certain items, such as chocolates, or beer bought at the supermarket, prices are probably what you would expect to pay at home.

WHERE TO SHOP

The main shopping street is Steenstraat, off the Markt, which has everything you would expect in the way of shops catering to everyday local needs, including clothes, shoes, food, home furnishings and electrical goods. There are also a few shops that sell Belgian chocolates and souvenirs. The street and its associated malls become very crowded on Saturday, when the best time to go is first thing in the morning.

Bruges' network of small city-centre streets and alleys conceals a surprising number of shops, most of them specialising in items such as lace, chocolate or clothes. Particular streets to look around are those surrounding the Burg and the Markt. Most of the city's squares have few shops: the

> ### Shopping hours
>
> Shopping hours are 9/10am–5.30/6pm; many smaller shops close for an hour at lunch time. Late-night shopping tends to be on Friday, with many stores open until 7–7.30pm. Shops that cater mainly to tourists, which in Bruges is just about all of them, usually open on Sunday.

Markt and the Burg are bounded by historical buildings with some cafés and restaurants; Jan van Eyckplein has none; and 't Zand is all bistros and hotels. An exception is Sint-Jansplein.

Bruges has a number of markets. The main one is on Wednesday on the Markt, and there is a bric-a-brac and craft market on 't Zand and Beursplein on Saturday (both open 8am–1pm). Don't miss the excellent antiques and flea market that takes place along the Dijver canal from 15 March to 15 November on Saturday and Sunday from 10am–6pm. A huge flea market is held three times a year (in August and September) in Koning Albertpark and 't Zand Square.

GOOD BUYS

Antiques. These are plentiful and are sold mostly in small, intimidatingly expensive-looking stores in the narrow side streets off the main shopping areas. An excellent example is Antiek Theatergalerij (Atelier Papageno, Vlamingstraat 52; tel: 050 33 05 94; www.antiek-vanmullem.be), which deals in restored old furniture, chandeliers and paintings.

Beer. This is an essential purchase for connoisseurs, with many brands on sale that are simply not available elsewhere. You will need a car to carry significant quantities. The range of Belgian beers is vast, so it is safest to stick to those you have tried and liked rather than risk being disappointed by an unknown. Note that it is much cheaper to buy beer at conventional supermarkets, but they may not stock your favourites.

Tax-free?

Tax-free shopping is available in stores that display the appropriate notice – usually the larger or more expensive specialised stores. If you're not sure, ask for details in the shop itself (see also page 128).

Exquisite handmade chocolates are everywhere

A good place to try in Bruges is the delicatessen Deldycke at Wollestraat 23 (tel: 050-33 43 35; www.deldycke.be), which stocks Bruges beers and 12-bottle selection crates.

Chocolate. 'Made in Belgium', probably the best in the world and available everywhere. It is best to avoid the tourist-oriented products, such as the chocolate rabbits, and concentrate on the incomparable delights of the classic, exquisite, handmade Belgian praline and truffle. Selection boxes (either pre-packed, or filled with your own choices) can be bought in a range of weights and are always attractively gift-wrapped.

A good shop in Bruges is Chocolatier Van Oost at Wollestraat 11 (tel: 050-33 14 54; www.chocolatiervanoost.net), a small store with a select range. Other fine outlets worth visiting are Pralinette, at Wollestraat 31B (tel: 050-34 83 83; www.pralinette.be), and The Chocolate Line, at Simon Stevinplein 19 (tel: 050-34 10 90; www.thechocolateline.be).

Jenever gin, known as Dutch gin by the English, is Belgium's national spirit

€ 17,36   € 17,36

Food and wine. Purchases may be limited by your tastes and appetites, the time of year, the freshness of the produce, or even the size of your car. But it would be a shame not to come away with something, even if it is just for your return journey. Belgium is justly celebrated for its pâtisseries and cakes, and there are some superb specialist food shops and delicatessens in Bruges. Pâtisserie Academie at Vlamingstraat 56 (tel: 050-68 92 91; www.patisserieacademie.be) has an equally delectable selection, while the aforementioned delicatessen Deldycke (at Wollestraat 23) has an excellent range of fine foods and wines.

Lace. Lace was once Bruges' principal product and is certainly the premier souvenir today. In the course of your strolls through the city you are likely to see enough lace shops to satisfy even the most ardent admirer of this delicate fabric. Although most lace on sale is machine-made, usually in the Far East, handmade lace in the distinctive *duchesse* (duchess), *bloemenwerk* (flower lace), *rozenkant* (pearled rosary), and *toveressesteek* (fairy stitch) styles can still be found. Some shops deal exclusively in the handmade product, which has a Quality Control label and is, of course, more expensive, but most shops sell a mix of the two. Breidelstraat (connecting the Markt with the Burg) is the city's lace alley, but it is sold throughout the city, so you will have plenty of choice. Reliable sources of guaranteed, authentic Belgian handmade lace are the family-run Lace Jewel, at Philipstockstraat 11 (tel: 050-33 42 25; www.bruges-shop.com), Melissa, Katelijnestraat 38 (tel: 050-33 45 32) and 't Apostelientje, Balstraat 11 (tel: 050-33 78 60; www.apostelientje.be).

ENTERTAINMENT

Walking, watching, eating and drinking are the chief pleasures of Bruges, but you can tour the city by boat and by horse-drawn carriage – peaceful and relaxing ways to see the sights (see page 122).

Bruges' café scene mainly takes place indoors, since space and city preservation rules allow little else (although tables do appear outside in the summer, and some pedestrianised squares, like handsome little Huidenvettersplein, provide exceptions to this rule).

Bookmark 4,50

Handmade Belgian lace

Bars and restaurants in the Markt

Bicycles are easy to rent (see page 112) and the city is flat, though you will have to cope with the cobblestones. From Bruges, you can easily cycle to Damme along the canal.

NIGHTLIFE

Music, opera, theatre. There are regular music festivals and concerts throughout the year; the city tourist office will have the latest information. Bruges has performances of classical music, opera and dance at the Concertgebouw, in 't Zand, and at the Stadsschouwburg, Vlamingstraat 29 (www.ccbrugge. be). Hotels and churches frequently host a variety of concerts and recitals.

Cinemas. International films are shown in their original language, with subtitles. The tourist office in Bruges can tell you what's on; the main cinema is Lumière in Sint-Jacobsstraat 36 (tel: 050-34 34 65; www.lumierecinema.be), while Liberty

in Kuipersstraat 23 (tel: 050-33 20 11; www.cinema-liberty.be)
has the occasional off-beat film.

Nightclubs. In Ghent, most clubs are to be found in the Zuid
Quarter, but Bruges has little to offer those who want to dance
the night away; it tends to be quiet at night. The Cactus Club,
Magdalenastraat 27 (tel: 050-33 20 14; www.cactusmusic.be),
in the suburb of Sint-Andries, is one of Bruges' most adventurous venues, with its electro-industrial and frontline-assembly
bands, as well as nostalgia events like rock-and-roll dances.

The lounge-bar at the chic brasserie-restaurant B-IN, in the
Oud Sint-Jan complex between Mariastraat and Zonnekemeers
(tel: 050-31 13 00; www.b-in.be), has regular DJ evenings. In
equally hip Lokkedize, Korte Vulderstraat 33(tel: 050-33 40 50;
http://bistrolokkedize.be/) one can hear jazz, blues and rock'n'
roll. The multipurpose venue De Werf, at Werfstraat 108 (tel:
050-33 0529, www.dewerf.be) in the northern harbour district, is
best known for good jazz and theatrical performances (in Dutch).

Bars. 't Brugs Beertje, Kemelstraat 5 (tel: 050-33 96 16;
www.brugsbeertje.be), a popular traditional café, has more
than 300 ales on its menu. Old World atmosphere is built
into the city's oldest tavern, Café Vlissinghe, Blekersstraat 2
(tel: 050-34 37 37; www.cafevlissinghe.be), which dates from
1515. If you are a fan of both Spanish tapas and the Blues,
you will find this some-
what unlikely combo at Vino
Vino, Grauwwerkersstraat
15 (tel: 0486 27 11 66).
At De Versteende Nacht,
Langestraat 11 (tel: 050-33
36 66), you can have a meal
and a drink, read comic
books (or look at them

Events guide

Bruges Tourist Office
issues a free publica-
tion, *events@brugge*
(http://events.brugge.be),
which lists entertainment
and events in the city.

– they're in Dutch) and listen to jazz from Bebop to modern. The music café Ma Rica Rokk, 't Zand 6–8 (tel: 050-33 24 34; www.maricarokk.be) is noisy enough to appeal to youthful spirits who can handle techno while they drink, while Delaney's at Burg 8 (tel: 050-34 91 45; www.delaneys.be) is an Irish bar-restaurant that has regular evenings of Irish music.

SPORTS

Switch on any hotel television and you will soon learn that football (soccer) is the top spectator sport. Bruges has its own football team, Club Brugge KV (www.clubbrugge.be), which is often a challenger for national and European honours, and plays its home games at the Jan Breydelstadion in the Sint-Andries district, to

Cycling in Bruges

the west of the historic centre of the city. It shares the stadium with the enthusiastic, but far less successful, local side Cercle Brugge (www.cerclebrugge.be).

Cycling is also popular here, and when you are in Bruges, you can obtain information about all aspects of sport and recreation from Sportdienst Brugge (tel: 050-72 70 00). Many sports facilities are in the suburbs, but are easily reached from the city centre. In Bruges, there are swimming pools in Sint-Kruis and Sint-Andries; in Ghent, the Centre Blaarmeersen offers swimming, squash, tennis and athletics.

ACTIVITIES FOR CHILDREN

Amusement parks. Boude-wijn Seapark at A. De Baeckestraat 12 (tel: 050-38 38 38; www.boudewijn park.be), includes a dol-phinarium with daily shows throughout the year, fair-

Old belfry bells in Bruges' Sound Factory

ground rides, and Bobo's Indoor, a play area. De Toverplaneet at Legeweg 88 (tel: 0478-22 69 29; www.detoverplaneet.be) is an indoor playground that is open Wednesdays, Fridays, weekends and public holidays. In Zeebrugge, a harbour-side theme park called **Seafront Zeebrugge** at Vismijnstraat 7 (www.seafront.be) is usually a winner.

Museums and attractions. Most museums in Bruges will only appeal to older children, but there are some exceptions. And if they have heads for heights, children should love climbing the Belfry.

Puppet theatre. In the second half of July Ghent hosts a Puppet Festival (www.puppetbuskersfestival.eu), with stages dotted around town, which is bound to appeal to younger children.

Tours. Canal boat tours and horse-drawn carriage rides are both popular with children, and you can rent bicycles of sizes to suit the whole family and explore at the children's pace.

CALENDAR OF EVENTS

For the most up-to-date information and for specific dates on the festivals and arts calendar in Bruges, consult the tourist office. The following list gives an idea of some of the major events taking place throughout the year.

April *Bruges:* Cinema Novo Film Festival, held at various venues across the city.

May *Bruges:* Heilig-Bloedprocessie – one of Belgium's most important historical and ecclesiastical pageants. The Dwars door Brugge road race is also held in May.

Ypres: Kattenstoet (Festival of the Cats) – a colourful medieval pageant that features cats (toy cats!) being thrown from the Belfry by the town jester; takes place every three years (next due in 2018).

July *Bruges:* Festival of Flanders (www.gentfestival.be) – a major festival of classical music that takes place over several months throughout Flanders; venues in Bruges include concert halls, churches and historic buildings; Cactus Festival – celebrating world music at Minnewater.

Ghent: Ghentse Feesten – a range of musical and cultural festivities take place in the city centre in a massive 10-day street festival.

August *Bruges:* Festival of the Canals – a nocturnal pageant along the illuminated canals that takes place every four years (next due in 2017). Early Music Festival, various venues. Pageant of the Golden Tree – commemoration once every five years of the wedding of Charles the Bold and Margaret of York (next due in 2017).

Ghent: Patershol Feesten – various festivities in the Patershol area of the city. International Chamber Music Festival at various venues.

Zeebrugge: Sand Sculpture Festival – stunning transformation of part of the Zeebrugge seashore into towering works of art.

August–September *Bruges:* Zandfeesten, the largest flea market in Flanders (held on Sundays on 't Zand).

October *Ghent:* International Film Festival.

November *Ghent:* Six Days of Ghent cycling event in Het Kuipke stadium.

December *Bruges:* Kerstmarkten – Christmas market and ice-rink on Markt and Simon Stevinplein. *Ghent:* Christmas market at Sint-Baafsplein.

EATING OUT

Belgians take their eating very seriously. Their rich cuisine and, of course, the *fritjes* are world famous. The quality is almost always excellent. Portions are generous; even if you ask for a sandwich, your plate will generally arrive loaded with much more than just garnish. Regional cuisines are strongly defined, but in the cities you should have no trouble sampling dishes from all over Belgium (and beyond).

RESTAURANTS AND BARS

Bruges and Ghent have a great many restaurants, cafés and bars from which to choose. 'Restaurant' can mean anything

from a formal, top-class establishment to a small café. Bars usually serve simple, hearty food at reasonable prices. Even in the smallest place you will be served at your table so, if in doubt, simply take your seat: most waiters are pleased to speak English.

Menus are often printed in a variety of languages, and at lunch (*middagmaal*) and dinner (*avondeten*) there is often a choice of set menus at fixed prices; these are the

Mussels, French fries and a local beer are a favourite meal

Bruges' dining scene caters to every taste.

best value. Most restaurants also offer a good-value dish of the day *(dagschotel)*. Bars and cafés usually serve snacks in the morning, then lunch from around noon; times and menus are posted in the windows. Many bars stay open until the early hours.

BREAKFAST

Some hotels serve substantial buffet breakfasts *(ontbijt)*, which can see you through until lunch time with no trouble at all, though it usually costs extra. Along with tea or coffee and fruit juice, there will be a variety of breads, cheeses and cold meats, plus fresh fruit and cereal, yogurt and fruit salads, buns and pastries. You may be asked if you would like a boiled egg, and some of the larger hotels also provide buffet grills, so you can have a fried breakfast as well. Even in the smaller hotels the choice and quality is very good.

COLD DISHES

A *boterham* is an open sandwich, which you will find served just about everywhere. Usually comprising two or three huge slices of bread with the filling of your choice plus a salad, they are excellent when accompanied by a Belgian beer – and offer great value. There is an enormous range, from salmon to meat to cheeses.

FISH AND SHELLFISH

The close proximity of the North Sea means that fish dominates most menus. Alas, the canals of Bruges and Ghent are now virtually lifeless, but freshwater fish are brought to the table from further afield.

One great favourite is fresh mussels *(mosselen)* in season (from Zeeland, in Holland), which are advertised everywhere when they are available, generally between mid-July and mid-February. Served simply with wedges of lemon, or cooked in a cream, white wine, or garlic and parsley sauce, they are a great delicacy and frequently arrive in a large pan from which diners help themselves. Mussels are best eaten with that other great Belgian staple, *frieten* (French fries).

Trout *(forel)* is another firm favourite, often served in a sauce of white wine, and eel *(paling)* crops up on menus a lot, frequently in thick sauces with herbs: *paling in 't groen* – green eel cooked with green herbs – is a speciality, as is *tomates-crevettes* – fresh tomatoes filled with *grijze gaarnalen* (grey shrimp) in Marie Rose sauce. Fresh sole *(zeetong)*

Extras

Value-added tax (BTW) is nearly always included in the bill (as is service charge), so there is usually no need to tip unless you want to. However, it is customary to leave at least the small change.

is mostly served grilled, while oysters, lobsters and crab are dressed in a variety of sauces. Many restaurants have a tank of lobsters or crabs on view to entice customers and prove the freshness of the produce.

The local coastline delivers other types of seafood, such as herring *(haring)*, mostly from Nieuwpoort, which may be lightly salted on the boat and eaten raw as *maatjes*. Herring are also popular – and delicious – when served smoked, steamed, marinated, or in a rich, red wine sauce *(bonne femme)*.

Fish can also feature in the traditional *waterzooi*, a delicately flavoured stew made with vegetables and fish (or sometimes chicken). *Waterzooi op Gentse wijze*, a dish orginating from Ghent, is always made with fish.

MEAT AND POULTRY

Game, pork and beef play a prominent part in the Flemish diet, alongside a variety of chicken dishes. *Stoofvlees* is a classic Belgian dish of beef casseroled in beer, with onions and herbs. There are steaks of fine quality, too, usually served with *frieten* (French fries).

You may also come across goose *(gans)*, first boiled and then roasted. Veal *(kalf)* and liver *(lever)* dishes are also widely available. During the game season, rabbit or hare cooked in Gueuze beer with onions and prunes *(konijn met pruimen)* appear on many menus, as well as rich pheasant dishes in thick sauces. *Everzwijn* is wild boar, which comes from the Ardennes, and has lots of flavour.

VEGETABLES AND SALADS

You will find *witloof* (chicory) on most menus, served in a ham and cheese sauce; *stoemp*, a mixture of mashed potatoes and other vegetables, is often served with sausages.

Salad *(sla, salade)* is very much an incidental on Belgian menus, where meat and fish rule supreme. Salads to look out for include the *liégoise*, which contains green beans and potatoes and is served luke-warm, and the *wallonie*, which features a combination of potatoes and bacon.

CHEESE

Cheese *(kaas)* comes in an enormous number of different types, most of them Belgian, Dutch or French. Belgium alone produces 300, including Trappist cheeses such as Orval and Chimay. Belgian Gouda and Remoudou are some of the better-known names. Meals traditionally end with cheese, so leave some room.

DESSERTS AND PÂTISSERIES

The Belgians love a good dessert, and the more chocolate and cream it has the better. *Ijs* (ice cream) and *slagroom* (whipped cream) are usually involved somewhere, perhaps oozing from pancakes or waffles. The ideal way to round off a meal of mussels and chips is with a *dame blanche* –vanilla ice cream and rich, hot chocolate sauce. The selection of cakes, fruit tarts, pastries, buns and biscuits available is immense.

Belgian Blue cattle produce quality beef

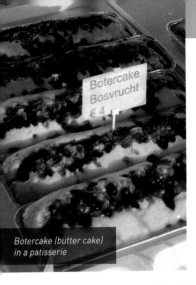

Botercake (butter cake)
in a patisserie

SNACKS

French fries are the staple snack of both Bruges and Ghent, sold from stalls and vans dotted around the streets. They can be topped with a variety of calorie-laden sauces: ketchup, mayonnaise, curry – you name it. There are fast-food places all over the towns; in Bruges, they are found mostly around the Markt, 't Zand and Steenstraat, and in Ghent you will see them in Vrijdagmarkt and the Veldstraat area.

Bars generally serve light snacks such as *Croque Monsieur* (toasted ham and cheese sandwich), plus filled rolls *(belegde broodje)*. Sweeter options include the doughy Liège and crispy Brussels waffles.

VEGETARIANS

Although the Belgian diet is dominated by fish and meat, it is not difficult to adhere to a varied vegetarian regime in Bruges and Ghent. However, this usually means foregoing traditional Flemish cooking. Listed in the Recommended Restaurants section are a number of places that serve vegetarian food. Be careful when ordering not to confuse vegetarian with *vleesgerecht*, which is a meat dish, and to remember also that the Belgian French fry *(friet)* is likely to have been cooked in animal fat. Some 'vegetarian' restaurants also serve meat and fish. If you cannot find a specialist establishment, head for one of the many Italian restaurants – non-meat pasta dishes and salads are usually offered as a matter of course.

DRINKS

Coffee *(koffie)* is fairly strong and usually served with extras such as little biscuits or chocolates, plus two or three kinds of sugar. Coffee liqueurs (especially Irish coffee) are popular and available everywhere. Tea *(thee)* is often served in a glass with lemon and without milk. Lipton-brand herbal teas are widely available.

Some of Belgium's many varieties of beer *(bier)* are described on page 102. Most bars stock at least 20 or 30, and a few will have more than 100. Those on tap *(van 't vat)* are cheaper than the bottled kind. All the usual spirits are available in generous measures. *Jenever* is the indigenous gin, and it is very strong. Most of the wine *(wijn)* is imported from France and Germany.

Essential bars to visit in Bruges are: 't Brugs Beertje at Kemelstraat 5, where the friendly and knowledgeable landlord will advise you on all aspects of his 300 or so beers; and De Garre, in the alley of the same name off Breidelstraat, which has a comfortable atmosphere and an impressive range of beers that includes its own brand. In Ghent, try Het Waterhuis aan de Bierkant, Groentenmarkt 9, a popular canalside bar with more than 100 beers on offer; Café Het Spijker (www.cafehetspijker.be), Pensmarkt 3–5, an underground 13th-century former leprosy shelter; and De Dulle Griet (www.dullegriet.be), Vrijdagmarkt 50, which has more than 250 types of beer, plus 1.5-litre (2.5-pint) elongated Kwak glasses on proud display.

☉ BELGIAN BEERS

Beer is to the Belgians what wine is to the French and, indeed, many Belgian beers complete the last stage of their fermentation in corked bottles. Several hundred different sorts are produced; each has a distinctive character and serving glass.

Lambic beers are wild beers, so called because their fermentation involves exposure to wild yeast. Many have a sour, apple-like taste, but these may have added fruit to impart the distinctive flavour. *Kriek*, a delicious cherry beer, comes in a round glass, while *Frambozen* beer is a pale pink raspberry brew served in a tall-stemmed glass. White beers like the popular Hoegaarden are cloudy and generally light and youthful in flavour.

The label *Trappist* refers to specialist beers brewed in monasteries. *Tripel* is a very strong beer that was served to the abbot and other important personages; the monks drank the *Dubbel*, while everyone else drank a watery version. *Trappist Leffe* is a strong, dark beer, slightly sweet and served in a bulbous glass.

Kwak (a strong, light-coloured beer) is served in a glass with a spherical base that sits in a wooden stand. The 1.5-litre (2.5-pint) glasses and stands are so valuable that customers must often give up a shoe to ensure they don't run off with them.

One of the strongest beers is the appropriately named *Delirium Tremens*, which can take you by surprise if you are not used to it. Another powerful, but delicious, beer is *Corsendonck Agnus Dei*.

Gueuze is a very quaffable, honey-coloured, sweet beer served in a straight glass; *Loburg*, a light-coloured beer served in a tall glass; *Hoegaarden Grand Cru*, a refreshing, coriander-based beer; *Rodenbach Grand Cru*, a red beer with a sharp apple taste; and *Bourgogne des Flandres*, a light, flavourful red beer.

TO HELP YOU ORDER

I'd like a/an/some... **Heeft u...**

beer bier
bread brood
coffee koffie
dessert nagerecht
fish vis
ice cream ijs
meat vleesgerecht
milk melk
pepper peper

potatoes aardappelen
salad sla, salade
salt zout
soup soep
sugar suiker
tea thee
vegetables groenten
water water
wine wijn

MENU READER

aardbei strawberry
appel apple
bonen beans
boter butter
eend duck
ei egg
garnalen prawns
ham ham
haring herring
honing honey
kaas cheese
kers cherry
kip chicken
koek cake
kool cabbage
kreeft lobster
lam lamb
macaroni noodles

mosselen mussels
nieren kidneys
oesters oysters
peer pear
perzik peach
pruim plum
ree venison
rijst rice
rode wijn red wine
rodekool red cabbage
rund beef
sinaasappel orange
snoek pike
taart flan
varken pork
witte wijn white wine
worst sausage
zalm salmon

PLACES TO EAT

Prices are for a three-course meal including tax but not drinks. The restaurants listed here accept all major credit cards unless otherwise stated.

€€€€ above 75 euros
€€€ 50–75 euros
€€ 25–50 euros
€ below 25 euros

BRUGES

Bhavani €€ *Simon Stevinplein 5; tel: 050-33 90 25; www.bhavani.be; Thu–Tue noon–2.30pm, 6–10pm.* If you want a change from Belgian food, good quality, authentic Indian cuisine is served here. Specialities are Madras and tandoori dishes; there are also vegetarian choices.

Pita Huis €€ *Philipstockstraat 35; tel: 050 67 76 11; Tue–Sun noon–2pm and 6–10pm;* This Mediterranean bar offers a nice selection of vegetarian and meat dishes including vegetarian lasagne, falafels, lamb and chicken gyros accompanied by a variety of sauces. Prices are reasonable, though the quality of service may be patchy.

Breydel-De Coninc €€ *Breidelstraat 24; tel: 050-33 97 46; http://restaurant-breydel.be; Thu–Tue noon–2.30pm, 6–9.30pm.* Conveniently located between the Burg and the Markt, this long-standing proponent of the Belgian obsession with mussels has traditional style and wood-beamed ceilings. It serves the mollusc in a variety of ways – the most popular of which is the basic big steaming potful – and all are worth going back for. Other seafood dishes, such as lobster and eels, have a place on the menu too.

De Belgede Boterham € *Kleine Sint-Amandsstraat 5; tel: 050-34 91 31; http://interior.debelegdeboterham.be; Mon–Sat 11.30am–4pm.* Friendly, small rustic wholefood café and pâtisserie just west of the Markt. The menu includes fresh Flemish sandwiches and salads.

Zet'Joe €€€€ *Langestraat 11; tel: 050 33 82 59; www.dekarmeliet.be; Closed Sun–Mon.* Indefatigable owner-chef Geert Van Hecke has created this recently opened restaurant after closure of the legendary De Karmeliet, which used to be just a few buildings up on the same street. Despite its ordinary name, the restaurant occupies a gastronomic class of its own. Beautiful interior is accompanied by excellent, though not cheap, haut-cuisine. Set menus range from €75 to €345 per person.

De Koetse €€ *Oude Burg 31; tel: 050-33 76 80; www.dekoetse-brugge. be; Sat–Wed noon–2.30pm, 6–10pm.* Inviting restaurant, just off Simon Stevinplein, with a rustic Flemish interior and a blazing fire in winter. It serves robust Flemish cooking, including spare ribs.

De Stove €€ *Kleine Sint-Amandsstraat 4; tel: 050-33 78 35; www. restaurantdestove.be; Mon–Tue and Fri–Sat from 7pm, Sun noon–2pm and 7–9pm.* An intimate restaurant with a 20-year reputation, just west of the Markt. Family-owned and operated, it specialises in Flemish dishes, with an emphasis on salads, fish and steaks.

De Visscherie €€€€ *Vismarkt 8; tel: 050-33 02 12; www.visscherie.be; Thu–Mon noon–2pm, 7–10pm.* With a name like this and a location in the Vismarkt (Fish Market) it is no surprise that the speciality here is seafood, and nowhere in town does it better. A modern interior is the setting for dishes served both nouvelle cuisine-style and in classic Belgian manner. Among the latter is a North Sea *waterzooi* (Flemish fish stew).

Den Dyver €€€ *Dijver 5; tel: 050-33 60 69; www.dyver.be; Tue–Sat 12– 2.30pm, 6–10pm.* On the main canal, close to the Groeningemuseum, this is one of the finest restaurants in Bruges and renowned for using Belgian beer in its recipes. It turns cooking into an art form.

Den Gouden Harynck €€€ *Groeninge 25; tel: 050-33 76 37; www. goudenharynck.be; Tue–Fri noon–2pm, 7–9pm, Sat 7–9pm.* An exceptionally fine restaurant just west of the Groeningemuseum that was once a fish shop (look for the sign of the herring). If there is such a thing as nouvelle Flemish cuisine, then this is where you will find it; the wine list is superb.

Die Swaene €€€ *Steenhouwersdijk 1; tel: 050-34 27 98; Thu–Mon noon–2pm, 6.30–9pm.* French/Flemish cuisine is served amid elegant surroundings in the very fine hotel of the same name, just off the Vismarkt.

Duc de Bourgogne €€€ *Huidenvettersplein 12; tel: 050-33 20 38; www. ducdebourgogne.be; Tue 7–9.30pm, Wed–Sun noon–2.30pm, 7–9.30pm.* A classic Bruges dining experience. Serves French dishes in baronial surroundings, with a canal view that is one of the city's most photographed.

Het Mozarthuys €€ *Huidenvettersplein 1; tel: 050-33 45 30; www.mozart huys.com; Mon–Thu, Sun 10am–10pm, Fri–Sat 10am–11pm.* Guess which famous composer's music wafts among the tables at this old-style Flemish restaurant? Yes, you can hum along to Wolfgang Amadeus while you enjoy its speciality grilled meat dishes and mussels. Lovely outdoor terrace in good weather.

Huidevettershuis €€ *Huidenvettersplein 10; tel: 050-33 95 06; www.huide vettershuis.be; Mon, Thu–Fri noon–2pm, 6–10pm, Sat–Sun noon–10pm.* An elegant canal-side eatery (the entrance is just off Vismarkt), specialising in Flemish cuisine. The building, which was formerly the Tanners' Guild House, dates from 1630. Closed Tuesday.

Le Pain Quotidien € *Philipstockstraat 21; tel: 050-33 60 50; www.lepain quotidien.be; Mon–Sat 7am–7pm, Sun 8am–6pm.* Fresh breads and cakes are on sale here. Go for breakfast, lunch or tea to revel in the family atmosphere. An enormous central table dominates the room. No credit cards.

Maximiliaan van Oostenrijk €€ *Wijngaardplein 16–17; tel: 050-33 47 23; www.maximiliaanvanoostenrijk.be; Thu–Tue 10am–10.30pm.* Burgundian restaurant in one of the most romantic parts of the city, adjacent to the Begijnhof. Specialities include the traditional local stew, *waterzooï*, grilled meats and seafood.

Patrick Devos €€€€ *Zilverstraat 41; tel: 050-33 55 66; Mon–Tue, Thu–Fri noon–1.30pm, 7–9pm, Wed noon–1.30pm, Sat 7–9pm.* Lavishly appointed restaurant, set in a 13th-century building that serves as a showplace for chef/ owner Patrick Devos' stunning creations using fresh regional produce.

Pietje Pek €€ *Sint-Jakobsstraat 13; tel: 050-34 78 74; www.pietjepek. com; Mon–Tue, Thu–Sun 5.30pm–midnight.* Behind its notable Art Nouveau façade, this restaurant serves satisfying portions of its speciality cheese and meat fondues, as well as an all-you-can-eat menu.

Spinola €€€ *Spinolarei 1; tel: 050-34 17 85; Tue–Sat noon–1.30pm, 7–9pm.* Spinola is a romantic, beautifully furnished restaurant just off the picturesque Jan van Eyckplein. The food is in a class that matches the surroundings, with fish dishes a speciality. The extensive wine list features as many as 300 wines.

Strijdershuis € *In the Hotel Koffieboontje, Hallestraat 14; tel: 050-33 80 27; www.strijdershuis.be; daily 10.30am–10pm.* This informal café-cum-restaurant situated just off the Markt is invariably crowded. The lively clientele is usually made up mostly of young backpackers, who are attracted by the extensive good-value set menus.

't Bourgoensche Cruyce €€€€ *Wollestraat 41–3; tel: 050-33 79 26; Thur–Mon noon–2.30pm, 7–9.30pm.* This is generally regarded as one of the best, most atmospheric dining experiences in Bruges, set in a beautiful old hotel overlooking the canal, serving Flemish regional specialities.

Tom Pouce €€ *Burg 17; tel: 050-33 03 36; daily 10am–11pm.* This is a large restaurant, but it manages not to be impersonal, and it enjoys an unrivalled position on the Burg. Although fish and Flemish cuisine dominate the menu, the quality of the food is secondary to that of the location. Order a waffle or pancake, sit on the heated outdoor terrace and watch the world go by.

GHENT

Avalon € *Geldmunt 32; tel: 09-224 37 24; www.restaurantavalon.be; Tue–Sat 11.30am–2.30pm.* Across the street from the Gravensteen fortress, Avalon offers tasty organic, vegetarian dishes such as home-made soup served with home-baked bread, and slices of savoury quiche. The antique-tiled main room is a protected monument; there is also an attractive little garden terrace.

Belfort Restaurant €€€ *Emile Braunplein 40; tel: 09-223 35 65; Tue–Sun 11.30am–2pm, 6–10pm.* Light, bright, open-plan restaurant right in the centre of town, beneath the eaves of the Stadshal. The open kitchen prepares posh versions of the Belgian classics.

Belga Queen €€€€ *Graslei 10; tel: 09-280 01 00; www.belgaqueen.be; daily noon–2.30pm, 6.30–10.30pm.* Stylish, even sexy, high-design restaurant inside a 13th-century grain storehouse, on Ghent's main section of canal. Fancy French/Belgian fare that is cheaper is you opt for the good-value midweek menus.

Brasserie HA' €€€ *Kouter 29; tel: 09-265 91 81; www.handelsbeurs.be; Mon–Sat 9am–10.30pm, Sun 9am–4pm.* Elegant yet cool, the Handelsbeurs Theatre's café-restaurant serves refined French and Belgian cuisine – light and breezy for lunch, candle-lit romantic for dinner. A multi-coloured modern chandelier graces the main dining room, and in the summer you can enjoy your meal seated on the lovely outside terrace overlooking the Ketelvaart canal.

Keizershof €€ *Vrijdagmarkt 47; tel: 09-223 44 46; www.keizershof. net; Tue–Sat 11.30am–10.30pm.* This large, rambling restaurant has so much space that even when it's full it won't seem crowded. Diners pile into hearty portions of Belgian and continental food, amid decor that features wooden ceiling beams, plain wood tables and fashionably tattered walls. In summer, there are outdoor tables in the courtyard.

La Malcontenta €€ *Haringsteeg 7–9; tel: 09-224 18 01; Mon–Sat 5.30pm–1am.* This Patershol-district restaurant serves one of the most specific of specialities – cuisine from the Canary Islands. This means plenty of fish, paella, *patatas arrugadas* (tiny new potatoes cooked in their skins in very salty water) and *mojo* sauce (made with olive oil, vinegar, garlic and coriander).

Le Grand Bleu €€€ *Snepkaai 15; tel: 09-220 50 25; www.legrandbleu. be; Wed–Sun noon–4.30pm, 7–midnight.* Set in a small Provençal-style house with a lovely terrace by the Leie, west of Sint-Pietersstation, this seafood specialist presents Mediterranean-influenced fish dishes and a wide range of lobster variations. A few succulent meat dishes are also on offer.

Pakhuis €€ *Schuurkenstraat 4; tel: 09-223 55 55; www.pakhuis.be; Mon–Thur noon–2.30pm, 6.30–11pm, Fri–Sat noon–2.30pm, 6.30pm–midnight.* Pakhuis is a lively brasserie south of the Sint-Niklaaskerk, offering good modern Flemish and Franco-Italian cuisine. Its setting inside a restored former warehouse is especially impressive. Oyster and seafood platters are the speciality of the house.

Patiron € *Sluizeken 30; tel: 09-233 45 87; www.patiron.be;Tue–Fri 11.30am–6pm.* A delightful bio café north of the city centre, where everything is made on the premises, including some hearty soups. The main speciality, however, is quiche, with more than 80 delicious varieties to choose from.

't Klaverblad €€€ *Corduwanierstraat 61; tel: 09-225 61 17; www.free-webs.com/tklaverblad; Mon, Thu–Sat 6–10.30pm, Sun noon–midnight.* While most of the neighbouring restaurants in the Patershol try to lure you with music, 'themed cuisine' and moderate prices, 't Klaverblad is unashamedly gastronomic and expensive. French food is prepared with a Flemish twist, for serious eaters who appreciate good food.

Vier Tafels €€ *Plotersgracht 6; tel: 09-225 05 25; http://viertafels. be;Wed–Sun noon–2pm, 6–10pm.* Located in one of the serpentine alleys of the Patershol district, this restaurant started with just four tables, hence its name. Now considerably enlarged, it has an adventurous menu of dishes from around the world.

A-Z TRAVEL TIPS

A SUMMARY OF PRACTICAL INFORMATION

A

ACCOMMODATION (see also Camping, Youth hostels, and the Recommended hotels chapter)

Bruges is particularly busy in the summer months, at Easter and at weekends, so it is advisable to book well in advance if you plan to visit at this time. If you are travelling in the low season or during the week, ask about discounts – many hotels do special deals from about October to March. The rates on page 135 are averages for double rooms in high season. Service charges and taxes are included. There is often a supplement for single rooms.

There is a star rating system (indicated in the tourist information literature and by the front door of the hotel), but the number of stars bears little relation to what you may get. Some four-star hotels may have certain facilities but not be very pleasant, while hotels further down the scale can be delightful. A few hotel exteriors and foyers look splendid, but this can be deceptive. Inspect rooms first if you can.

A substantial breakfast is sometimes included in the hotel rate, but more often hotels now charge extra. This can add considerably to the price, so it may be worth looking for a local café that serves a good breakfast. The Bruges tourist office also supplies a list of bed-and-breakfast accommodation in its brochure.

The tourist offices in Bruges and Ghent can provide detailed lists of hotels in each city that describe facilities, prices and contact detail. You can also find them at Bruges official tourist website, www.visitbruges.be. They can also book rooms for you on payment of a deposit, which is then deducted from your hotel bill. If you arrive in either city without a room, try this service first.

How much per night/week? **Hoeveel kost het per nacht/ week?**

In Bruges, contact In & Uit ('t Zand 34; tel: 050-44 46 46, email: toerisme@brugge.be; www.visitbruges.be). Please note that as of 2014, the city of Bruges charges a €2 tourism tax per person (over 18) per night.

AIRPORT

Brussels Airport (BRU) (tel: 0900-70-000 in Belgium, tel: +32 2-753 77 53 from outside Belgium; www.brusselsairport.be) is located in Zaventem, 13km (9 miles) from the centre of the capital and served by most major airlines. It has all the facilities you would expect of an international airport.

There are train, bus and taxi connections from the airport to Brussels – the train links are the most efficient, running every 15 minutes at peak times from the airport to all three of Brussels' main stations. From these there are regular train links to Bruges and Ghent; the travel time from Brussels is about an hour to Bruges and 30 minutes to Ghent.

The trip by taxi from the airport to the centre of Brussels will cost you substantially more than the train, but a reduction in the taxi fare is available if you present a round-trip air ticket.

B

BICYCLE RENTAL

Bruges encourages cyclists by allowing them to travel down more than 50 one-way streets in either direction. It's not as dangerous as it sounds, due to the special cycle lanes. The Bruges tourist office and website has a full list of which establishments rent bikes. Some hotels put bikes at their guests' disposal; ask when you arrive. They can be hired from the railway station in Bruges and other towns by the day. A discount is offered if you present a valid train ticket. Bikes can be left at other participating rail stations – an information leaflet is available from sta-

I'd like to hire a bicycle **Ik wil graag een fiets huren**

tions. Among other hire locations in Bruges are Hotel Koffieboontje at Hallestraat 4 (tel: 050-33 80 27), Fietsen Popelier at Mariastraat 26 (tel: 050-34 32 62), and Bruges Bike Rental at Niklaas Desparsstraat 17 (tel: 050-61 61 08; www.brugesbikerental.be).

BUDGETING FOR YOUR TRIP

Bruges can be expensive, but no more so than other popular European tourist destinations, and less so in many respects than Belgium's capital, Brussels.

Getting to Belgium. The cost of getting to Belgium from the UK and Ireland by air varies considerably. Flying with Ryanair one way from various airports in both countries to Brussels-Charleroi Airport can cost only a few pounds or euros (plus taxes and other charges), but £20–40 (€24–€48) one way is probably nearer the average, and can easily go higher. These rates have forced carriers such as BA, BMI, Aer Lingus and Brussels Airlines to cut their fares for flights into Brussels Airport.

Of the other options, going by bus from London to Bruges is likely to be the cheapest. By train, Eurostar from London St Pancras Station to Brussels offers excursion and advance-purchase tickets, as does the Channel Tunnel car-transporter. The cost of going by ferry from Britain (departing from Hull) to Zeebrugge varies considerably depending on the route, whether travelling as a foot passenger or with a car, and whether you want a cabin. For foot passengers, the price varies from about £100 one-way in low season, to about £300 in high.

Accommodation. For a double room with en-suite bathroom and breakfast in Bruges you can pay around €60, but for reasonable comfort and facilities, €75–100 is a more realistic starting point; a mid-range hotel will cost €100–200; and expensive hotels begin at about €200. What you get obviously varies with the location and the time of year. At the busiest times – and Bruges is very often busy – rooms can be hard to come by.

Eating out. You can eat well in many of Bruges' restaurants for about €30 per person for a three-course meal without wine. However, a more realistic starting point would be €25–50; in mid-range establishments, expect to pay €50–75; and in an expensive restaurant, more than €75. If you are on a tight budget look for the *dagschotel* (dish of the day) or the *dagmenu* (menu of the day), available in most restaurants, which will offer a worthwhile saving. Alternatively, eat in a café (bar) that serves low-cost food – this could be a simple spaghetti bolognese or *biefstuk met frieten/steak-friet* (steak and fries).

Museums. Public museums charge €4–8 for adult admission, while privately owned attractions may cost up to €12; save money by buying a Musea Bruges Pass (see page 25). There are reduced rates for children, senior citizens and students.

Public transport. A single ticket covering the city costs €3 if bought before boarding; €2 if you buy it on your mobile and is valid for 60 minutes. A one-day pass costs €6 if bought before boarding, and €8 on board the bus; multi-day passes are available. For details see www.delijn.be.

C

CAMPING

Belgium's campsites are graded from one to four stars and are usually excellently equipped. There is just one campsite in Bruges that is close enough to permit easy use of public transport into the city centre, though there are others farther away, and along the Belgian coast. Camping Memling (Veltemweg 109, 8310 Bruges; tel: 050-35 58 45; www.bruges camping.be) is in the Sint-Kruis district in the east of the city.

The tourist office will provide a camping leaflet on request. It is advisable to book pitches in advance during the high season. Spending the night in cars, caravans, mobile homes or tents by the roadside, in woods, dunes or directly on the beach is forbidden.

CAR HIRE (see also Driving)

With a city centre as compact as that of Bruges, a well-organised public transport bus system, and strict rules regulating parking, there is no need for a car in the city. If you want to explore the countryside around

Bruges, to include the nearby coast and World War I battlefields around Ypres, you may want to hire a car for a day or two. Major car hire firms are represented in the city, and there are many local firms whose contact details you can find in the *Gouden Gids (Yellow Pages)*. If time permits you should compare prices.

The minimum age may be 20 or 25, depending on the company and the vehicle. Credit cards are almost always required for payment, and you will need to show your driving licence and passport.

Many hotels have arrangements with car hire companies that make it simple to arrange for a car, but a small extra charge will normally be made for delivery to your hotel.

Avis, Bevrijdingslaan 37, tel: 050-39 44 00, www.avis.com/en/locations/be/brugge.

Europcar, Sint-Pieterskaai 48, tel: 050-31 45 44, www.europcar.com/location/belgium/bruges/bruges.

Hertz, Pathoekeweg 25, tel: 050-37 72 34, www.hertz.com.

CLIMATE

Belgium has a temperate climate much influenced by its proximity to the sea, although obviously this influence diminishes inland. The warmest and driest weather is between April and October, but it can rain at any time of the year. Approximate monthly temperatures in Bruges are shown below. You can obtain a current weather forecast at www.meteo.be.

	J	F	M	A	M	J	J	A	S	O	N	D
°C	5	6	10	13	19	21	23	22	20	14	8	6
°F	41	43	50	55	66	70	74	72	68	57	46	41

CLOTHING

The unpredictable climate means you should be prepared for rain at any time of the year. A raincoat is advisable, although many upmarket hotels provide complimentary umbrellas. In March and April, the weather can be bright and reasonably warm, but with sudden blasts of cold wind as you turn a corner; so a light coat that can be slipped on and off is a good idea. In winter, heavy coats and sweaters are advisable. Bruges is a walking city, so take comfortable, reliable shoes that you know will not hurt your feet, and take care on the cobblestones.

Dress is generally smart but relaxed and informal, although expensive restaurants will expect male guests to wear ties.

CRIME AND SAFETY (see also Police)

Its compactness and the numbers of tourists wandering its streets make Bruges extremely safe: you are seldom alone or far from the centre. There is very little crime, though obviously it makes sense to take elementary precautions with cameras, bags and personal effects. Valuables should be left in your hotel safe.

Ghent is very safe, too, but it is wise to stay clear of the small red-light district between Keizer Karelstraat and Vlaanderenstraat, and the area around Sint-Pietersstation late at night.

If you are planning to venture far into outlying areas of either city late at night, your hotel receptionist should be able to advise you on any areas best avoided.

D

DISABLED TRAVELLERS

Facilities, accessibility to transport, and buildings in both cities are distinctly patchy. The cobblestone streets and medieval buildings of Bruges mean access to some places of interest can be challenging, particularly as ramps and railings are invariably absent. Some hotels have ramps, but planning rules for older hotels forbid the installation of lifts (elevators), so some or all of the rooms can only be reached by the staircase. Museums are often similarly restricted, and may involve numerous stairs. Detailed information is included in the excellent brochure available online at: www.visitbruges.be/bruges-accessible-to-everyone-brochure.

Some of the larger (chain) hotels have specially designed rooms for guests with disabilities. There are, at most, usually two or three such rooms per hotel.

The new De Lijn buses are equipped with a low floor, ramp and hydraulic lifting device. They provide marked places reserved for disabled passengers, which are at the front of the bus by at the wheelchair accessible door. More details can be found on the De Lijn website: www.delijn.be/en. At some major road crossings in both cities, textured soft paving has been installed. All travellers should be careful near the canals, which often are not railed off from the footpath or road.

Bruges tourist information office produces a map showing free parking facilities for drivers with disabilities. Access Info (tel: 070 23 30 50; www.accessinfo.be), a branch of the Flemish Tourist Board, also has updates on disabled access. In the UK, information may be obtained from Tourism for All (tel: 0845-124 9971; www.tourismforall.org.uk).

In the US, contact the Society for the Advancement of Travel for the Handicapped (sath), tel: 212-447 7284, www.sath.org.

DRIVING (see also Car hire)

To take your car into Belgium, you will need:

International driving licence or your own national licence (held for at least a year).

Car registration papers.

Green Card (this does not provide cover, but is internationally recognised proof that you have insurance – not obligatory for EU countries).

Fire extinguisher, red warning triangle and reflective jacket in case of breakdown.

National identity sticker for your car, or an EU licence plate.

Headlight adaptors for right-hand-drive vehicles, to prevent the lights dazzling oncoming drivers.

Warning triangle and reflective vest.

Driving conditions. Drive on the right, pass on the left. Though you may wish to drive to and from Bruges, it is unnecessary and ill-advised to drive within the city itself. Bruges has a complex one-way system, with narrow winding roads that in high season are clogged with pedestrians, bicycles and horse-drawn carriages. Driving in Ghent is more aggressive than in Bruges and is made more complicated by the presence of trams, which you are not allowed to overtake and to which you must give way.

Belgium's motorway system is excellent, but it and the city ring-roads (like that in Bruges) can get clogged at rush hour. Other main roads in Flanders are generally very straight and free of traffic.

Rules of the road. Seat belts must be worn by both driver and passengers and there are stiff penalties for speeding and drink driving. Some offences require payment of fines on the spot.

An important rule to remember is that drivers should normally yield to traffic approaching from the right. A yellow diamond-shaped sign with a white border indicates that drivers on main roads have the right of way. When the sign reappears with a diagonal line through it, then drivers must yield to traffic from the right.

Speed limits. On motorways, the limit is 120km/h (75mph) and on other main roads it is 90km/h (55mph) in Wallonia and Brussels, and 70km/h (44mph) in Flanders. In residential areas the speed limit drops to 50km/h (30mph) or even 30km/h (18mph).

Parking. There is limited parking in the city centres. Larger car and coach parks exist around the perimeter of Bruges and on the edge of Ghent's pedestrian zone; it is safer (and quicker) to use them and walk into the centre. Both tourist offices provide maps indicating car parks.

Breakdown. Belgium's two main motoring organisations are the Touring Club de Belgique (www.touring.be) and the Royal Automobile Club de Belgique (www.racb.com). They have reciprocal arrangements with

rechtdoor straight ahead
links left
rechts right
op/om de hoek on/around the corner
bij het stoplicht at the traffic light
voorrang verlenen yield
benzine gas (petrol)
loodvrij unleaded
normaal regular
Fill it up, please **Vol, alstublieft**
Is this the right road to...? **Is dit de juiste weg naar...?**
I have a puncture/flat tyre **Ik heb een lek/lekke band**
My car broke down **Ik heb autopech**

other national motoring organisations. Motorways have emergency phones positioned at regular intervals. In case of breakdown, call Wegenhulp/Touring Secours, tel: 070-34 47 77.

Fuel and oil. Service stations are plentiful, and most international brands of unleaded *(loodvrij)* petrol (gasoline) and diesel are on sale.

Road signs. International pictographs are widely used, but here are some written signs you may encounter:

E

ELECTRICITY

Belgium operates on 230 volts, 50 Hz AC, requiring standard two-pin round continental plugs. Visitors should bring their own adapters.

EMBASSIES AND CONSULATES

All the foreign embassies and consulates are in Brussels.

Australia: Kunstlaan 56, 1000 Brussels; tel: 02 286 05 00; http://bel

gium.embassy.gov.au/

Canada: Kunstlaan 58, 1000 Brussels; tel: 02 741 06 11; www.canadain ternational.gc.ca/belgium-belgique/

New Zealand: Avenue des Nervien 9-31, 1040 Etterbeek; tel: 02 512 1040; www.mfat.govt.nz/en/countries-and-regions/europe/belgium/new-zea land-embassy

Republic of Ireland: Rue Froissart 50, 1040 Brussels; tel: 02 282 34 00; www.dfa.ie/irish-embassy/belgium/

South Africa: Rue Montoyer 17-19, 1000 Brussels; tel: 02 285 44 00; www.southafrica.be/

UK: Avenue d'Auderghem 10, 1040 Brussels; tel: 02 287 82 11; www.gov. uk/government/world/uk-representation-to-the-eu

US: Boulevard du Régent 27, 1000 Brussels; tel: 02 811 40 00; https:// be.usembassy.gov/

EMERGENCIES (see also Health and Police)

The three-digit emergency telephone numbers listed below are valid throughout Belgium:

General emergency number 112

Police assistance: 101

> I need an English-speaking doctor/dentist **Ik zoek een dokter/tandarts die Engels spreekt**

G

GAY AND LESBIAN TRAVELLERS

For information on the gay, lesbian and bisexual scene in Bruges, con-tact Jong & Holebi in Brugge (Koningin Elisabethlaan 92; tel: 050-33 69 70; www.j-h.be). For gay-friendly hotels and B&Bs use EBAB (www. ebab.com), a specialist accommodation search engine.

GETTING THERE

By air. Brussels Airport is linked by direct flights with major airlines from all European and many North American cities, but other long-distance travellers may have to connect via Amsterdam, London or Paris. Brussels Airlines (tel: 02-723 23 62; www.brusselsairlines.com), is the main local carrier. British Airways (tel: 0844-493 0787 in the UK; tel: 02-717 32 17 in Belgium; www.britishairways.com) flies from several UK airports to Brussels; flight time from London is about one hour. Several other airlines fly from UK airports to Brussels. They include Air France (tel: 0207 660 0337in the UK; tel: 070-22 24 66 in Belgium; www.airfrance.co.uk), KLM (tel: 020-7660 0293 in the UK; tel: +32 2 620 0220in Belgium; www.klm.com). Aer Lingus (tel: 0333 004 5000 in the UK; tel: 070-35 99 01 in Belgium; www.aerlingus.com) has regular service to Brussels from Dublin and Cork. Ryanair (tel: 0871-246 000 in the UK; tel: 1520 444 004 in Ireland; tel: 0902-33 660 in Belgium; www.ryanair.com) flies from airports in Britain and Ireland to Charleroi, near Brussels.

By rail. Brussels and Bruges have excellent rail connections with the rest of the European network. There are various discounts for EU residents, and it is best to contact your local rail operator for the latest information before your trip.

From the UK it is possible to reach Bruges and Ghent easily using the Eurostar service through the Channel Tunnel. Trains depart from St Pancras International in London or Ashford International in Kent and arrive in Brussels within one hour 50 minutes. You can be in Bruges or Ghent in just over three hours. Allow time for going through customs at St Pancras. Trains start boarding 20 minutes before they leave. Your bags stay with you at all times, so there is no delay waiting for luggage once you arrive. Trains are comfortable, and there is a well-stocked café/bar on board. Don't forget your passport.

Seats can be chosen and reserved when booking your ticket online (tel: 03432-186 186, www.eurostar.com), or at some mainline stations and travel agents.

If you want to take your car, Eurotunnel (tel: 08443-353 535, www.eurotunnel.com) trains travel via the Channel between Folkestone and Calais every 15 minutes. Passengers stay with their car for the 35-minute journey.

By bus. Eurolines (tel: 0871 781 8177 in the UK; tel: 02-274 13 50 in Belgium; www.eurolines.com) operates bus services between all major European cities and Brussels; those coming from London generally stop in Bruges.

By boat. There are car ferry crossings daily to Belgium from the UK (Hull to Zeebrugge) with P&O Ferries (tel: 0800 130 0030 in the UK; tel: +32 2 808 50 20 in Belgium; www.poferries.com).

GUIDES AND TOURS

Guided tours allow you to explore parts of the city that you might not discover on your own. Groups and individuals can book qualified and very informative guides in advance from the tourist office, for a minimum two-hour tour. Daily guided tours of the city, starting from the tourist office. For details, see www.visitbruges.be/practical-information.

Bruges's canals can be explored from 10am–6pm daily March–mid-November. Boats depart from Rozenhoedkaai, Dijver and Mariastraat. Night tours for groups can also be arranged on request, and can be very appealing. It can be chilly on these tour boats, and even on a warm summer day you may be grateful for a sweater or jacket.

A 50-minute tour round Bruges by bus with recorded commentary in the language of your choice makes a good introduction to the city. Tours are operated by City Tour (tel: 050-35 50 24; www.citytour.be), with minibuses departing from the Markt every 30 minutes. The same line runs two-hour tours to Damme, depending on the season: they also depart from the Markt and can include a free drink and pancake in Damme, and a return canal trip on the Lamme Goedzak paddle-boat.

Quasimodo (tel: (0) 800 97525; www.quasimodo.be) run minibus tours of the country-side and Flanders Fields, including a beer-and-waffle-themed itinerary. Horse-drawn carriage rides through the city centre depart from the Markt (occasionally from the Burg), with a 10-minute break for the horse at Minnewater.

Quasimundo (tel: 050-33 07 75; www.quasimundo.eu) – not to be confused with the Quasimodo above – runs cycling tours in and around Bruges. Tours, which last two hours and 30 minutes, include provision of a mountain bike, guide, transport by bus, insurance and rain gear.

H

HEALTH AND MEDICAL CARE (see also Emergencies)

Travellers from EU countries should receive free medical treatment in Belgium on presentation of the European Health Insurance Card (EHIC), available from post offices or online (www.ehic.org.uk), but it is wise to take out extra travel insurance, which should cover illness, accident and lost luggage. For non-EU citizens, travel insurance is essential.

A Belgian pharmacy (apotheek) is identified by a green cross and should have a list in the window of nearby late-night chemist shops. Such lists are also published in the local weekend press.

Call police or tourist information office for telephone numbers of doctors on weekend and night duty.

For a hospital in Bruges, go to the AZ Sint-Jan (Ruddershove 10; tel: 050-45 21 11; www.azsintjan.be).

Where's the nearest pharmacy (chemist)? **Waar is de dichtstbijzijnde apotheek?**

L

LANGUAGE

In Flanders, which covers roughly the northern half of Belgium, residents speak Flemish (a dialect of Dutch) and this is the language you hear in Bruges and Ghent. French is the language of Wallonia, southern Belgium. Brussels is officially bilingual, but has more French than Dutch speakers. A German-speaking minority of around 70,000 lives in the eastern districts of the country.

Hello/hi **Dag/hallo**
Good morning **Goedemorgen**
Good afternoon **Goedemiddag**
Good evening **Goedenavond**
What's your name? **Hoe heet u?**
My name is... **Mijn naam is...**
Goodbye/see you soon **Dag/tot ziens**
Yes **Ja**
No **Nee**
I'd like... **Ik wil graag...**
How much? **Hoeveel kost het?**
Where is/are...? **Waar is/zijn...?**
Please **Alstublieft**
Thank you **Dank u wel**
Days and Numbers
Monday **Maandag**
Tuesday **Dinsdag**
Wednesday **Woensdag**
Thursday **Donderdag**
Friday **Vrijdag**
Saturday **Zaterdag**
Sunday **Zondag**
0 **nul**
1 **één**
2 **twee**

3 **drie**
4 **vier**
5 **vijf**
6 **zes**
7 **zeven**
8 **acht**
9 **negen**
10 **tien**
11 **elf**
12 **twaalf**
13 **dertien**
14 **veertien**
15 **vijftien**
16 **zestien**
17 **zeventien**
18 **achttien**
19 **negentien**
20 **twintig**

Communications

Where's an internet café? **Waar vind ik een internetcafe?**

How much per hour/half hour? **Hoeveel kost het per uur/ half uur?**

Does it have wireless internet? **Is er draadloos internet?**

What is the WiFi password? **Wat is het wifi wachtwoord?**

Is the WiFi free? **Is wifi gratis?**

Are you on Facebook/Twitter? **Bent u op Facebook/ Twitter?**

English is spoken by many and should be at least partially understood by virtually everybody. Written and spoken Dutch contains many English loanwords and can sound familiar; at other times there are no clues as to meaning. Menus may be printed in English as well as Dutch and French; if they are not, most members of staff will be happy to explain what things mean.

Although local road signs are in Dutch, be aware that in this bilingual country many towns bear different names in French: Brugge (Dutch) is *Bruges* in French, Gent is *Gand*, Ieper is *Ypres*, Oudenaarde is *Audenarde*, and Antwerpen is *Anvers*.

M

MAPS

Bruges' tourist office produces a free comprehensive map of central Bruges, and several commercial maps can be bought at bookshops and newsagents around town.

MEDIA

Newspapers and magazines

English-language publications are sold at station kiosks, larger bookshops and newsstands. Larger hotels may stock the *International Herald Tribune*, *Financial Times* and other international newspapers.

Have you any English newspapers? **Heeft u Engelse kranten?**

Radio and television

BBC long-wave and world services and European-based American networks can be picked up easily. Most hotels have cable television with up to 30 channels, including BBC World News from the UK and CNN International from the US. Many European channels show English-language films (around 9pm) and programmes with subtitles.

MONEY

Currency

The unit of currency in Belgium is the euro, which is abbreviated to € and divided into 100 cents. Coins are: €2, €1, and 50, 20, 10, 5, 2 and 1 cents. Banknotes are in denominations of €500, 200, 100, 50, 20 10 and 5. The €500 and €200 notes are rarely if ever seen in circulation, and some small businesses may even be reluctant to accept €100 notes.

> I'd like to change some dollars/pounds into euros. **Ik wil graag wat dollars/ponden in euro's omwisselen.**
> Do you accept travellers' cheques? **Accepteert u reischeques?**
> Can I pay by credit card? **Kan ik met een creditcard betalen?**

Exchange facilities

There is a standard commission for changing foreign currency and travellers' cheques. Generally, banks offer the best rates, followed by bureaux de change. Hotels will often exchange currency, but at an inferior rate. Currency-exchange machines at Brussels Airport make transactions in several currencies. ATMs accepting non-Belgian debit and credit cards are widely available..

Credit cards

Major hotels and many restaurants and shops accept payment by international credit cards.

Travellers' cheques

These are still accepted in some places, but the practice is in decline. Cheques can be cashed as long as you show your passport.

Sales tax, service charge

Called BTW, a sales (value-added) tax is imposed on most goods and services in Belgium. In hotels and most restaurants, this is accompanied by a service charge. Both charges are included in the bill. To recover some of the tax on expensive purchases, look for shops displaying signs saying 'Europe Tax-Free Shopping' or 'Tax-Free International'; retailers are well acquainted with the necessary procedures.

O

OPENING TIMES

Banks open Monday–Friday 9am–noon, 2–4pm and some until 5pm. Some banks open on Saturday morning and until 6pm on one or two days a week.

Shops and department stores are generally open Monday–Saturday 10am–6 or 6.30pm and on the first Sun of each month ('Shopping Sunday').

Post offices are open Monday–Friday 9am–6pm. Larger post offices are also open on Saturday 9am–3pm.

Museums are generally open Tuesday to Sunday from 9.30 or 10am to 5pm (most close for lunch at midday). In Bruges, some may be closed on Tuesday or Wednesday during the low season.

P

POLICE (see also Emergencies)

The *politie* or police can be reached on the emergency 101 phone number. They are not that noticeable on the streets (there is seldom any need for them in Bruges), but they are usually dressed in dark blue. Any

Where's the police station? **War is het politiebureau?**

theft should be reported at the nearest police station. The main police station in Bruges is at Lodewijk Coiseaukaai 3, tel: 050-44 88 44.

POST OFFICES

The main post office in Bruges is on Smedenstraat 57, tel: 022 01 23 45; www.post.be; Mon–Fri 9am–6pm, Sat 9am–3pm. There are post offices in Ghent at Lange Kruisstraat 55. Smaller post offices close for lunch from noon until 2pm.

> A stamp for this letter/postcard, please. **Een postzegel voor deze brief/ansichtkaart, alstublieft.**
> I want to send this package by airmail/express. **Ik wil dit pakje per luchtpost/expres versturen.**

Mailboxes are red, often decorated with a white bugle. They may be either freestanding or attached to walls. Stamps can also be purchased from souvenir shops selling postcards.

PUBLIC HOLIDAYS

Most shops and other businesses are closed on public holidays; if museums are not closed, they will be operating on Sunday hours. If a holiday falls on a Sunday, the following Monday will usually be taken off instead.

1 January *Nieuwjaar* New Year's Day
1 May *Dag van de Arbeid* Labour Day
11 July *Feest van de Vlaamse* Flanders Day
21 July *Nationalefeestdag* National Day
15 August *Maria Hemelvaart* Assumption
1 November *Allerheiligen* All Saints' Day
11 November *Wapenstilstand* Armistice Day
25 December *Kerstdag* Christmas Day

Moveable dates:
Pasen Easter
Paasmaandag Easter Monday
Hemelvaartsdag Ascension Day
Pinkstermaandag Whit Monday

R

RELIGION

Belgium's population is predominantly Roman Catholic, but Protestant churches are also well represented in both cities. In Bruges, there is an English-language Anglican service held at Saint Peter's Chapel at Keersstraat 1, Sunday 6pm.

T

TELEPHONES

The phone system in Belgium is reliable and extensive. Hotel phones are the most convenient, although they are also the most expensive. Public phone booths are plentiful, particularly in the city centres and railway stations; most of them can be used to phone direct overseas, and have instructions in English, French and German as well as Dutch. Many booths only accept phonecards rather than coins: cards can be purchased from post offices, newsstands and railway stations.

The dialling code for Belgium is 0032; Brussels is 02, Bruges is 050, and Ghent is 09; you always need to use the local area code, even if you are calling from inside the area. The Yellow Pages directory *(Gouden Gids)* has a useful English-language index.

TIME ZONES

The following chart shows the time difference between Belgium and various cities in winter. Between the beginning of April and the end of October, Belgian clocks are put forward one hour.

New York	London	**Belgium**	Jo'burg	Sydney	Auckland
6am	11am	**noon**	1pm	10pm	midnight

TIPPING

In a country where service is included in most bills, tipping is not a problem. Most people will not expect a tip (but will appreciate it if you give them one). Exceptions include public toilets, where the attendant may expect a tip of 35–50 cents, and porter and maid service in the more expensive hotels.

TOILETS

A toilet is generally called a WC (pronounced vay-say) in Flanders. If there is not a graphic of some kind that leaves no room for doubt about which toilet is for females and which for males, look for the words *dames* (women) and *heren* (men). In small cafés and restaurants, men's and women's toilets may be only notionally separated.

TOURIST INFORMATION

Canada: English-speaking residents can contact the New York office, and by calling tel: +1-514 457 2888.

US: Belgian Tourist Office, 300 East 42nd Street, 14th floor New York, NY 10017; tel: 212 758 8130; www.visitbelgium.com

UK: Tourism Flanders-Brussels, Flanders House, 1a Cavendish Square, London W1G OLD; tel: 020 7307 7738; www.visitflanders.com

The main information office in Bruges is in the Concertgebouw, 't Zand 34 (tel: 050-44 46 46; email: toerisme@brugge.be, www.visitbruges.be; Mon–Sat 10am–5pm, Sun 10am–2pm). There is also a tourist information office near the station, at Stationsplein, as well as at Markt 1 inside the Historium museum (see page 27), where you can book hotel accommodation in the city.

The free monthly newsletter, *Exit*, and brochure, *events@brugge* (in

> Where is the tourist office? **Waar is het toeristen-bureau?**

English), are available from the tourist offices. *Exit* is only published in Dutch, but performance dates and venue details are fairly easy to understand.

In Ghent, the tourist office is located inside the renovated Oude Vismijn at Sint-Veerleplein 5 (tel: 09-266 56 60, email: visit@gent.be, www. visitgent.be, 15 March–14 October daily 9.30am–6.30pm, 15 October–14 March daily 9.30am–4.30pm).

TRANSPORT

In the city, where everything seems to be a short walk away, public transport is not usually a problem.

Buses

In Bruges, buses to the suburbs can be caught most conveniently in the Markt or at the railway station. Sightseeing buses and excursions also depart from the Markt. Other main bus stops are at Wollestraat, Biekorf and Kuipersstraat. A one-day pass (€6 if bought before boarding, €8 on board the bus) allows unlimited travel on all the city's buses. Regional buses (to destinations outside Bruges) can be caught at the railway station and in 't Zand. A helpline is available for both

> When's the next bus/train to...? **Wanneer vertrekt de volgende bus/trein naar...?**
> I want a ticket to... **Ik wil graag een kaart naar...**
> A one-way/return-trip ticket **Enkeltje/retourtje**
> A first-class/economy-class ticket **Kaartje eerste klas/ tweede klas**

types of bus on 070-22 02 00, and schedules are also displayed in the tourist information office.

In Ghent, the main bus station is outside Sint-Pieters railway station. This is also a terminus for many of the city's trams, which serve most of Ghent and are great fun to ride. Buses and trams can also be caught from the city centre, at Korenmarkt. The coastal tram (www.delijn.be) is an excellent way to explore the Flemish coast.

Taxis

Taxis are plentiful in both Bruges and Ghent, where they flock together outside the railway stations for the hotel run. Order your taxi at the hotel when you check out, and one will arrive in two or three minutes. However, taxis are rather more difficult to hail in the streets – in Bruges, you are most likely to find one in the Markt, while in Ghent the best place to try hailing a taxi is Korenmarkt.

Trains

The Belgian railway network is superb. Bruges and Ghent are situated on the same line that connects Brussels with Ostend. Train services are prompt and frequent. Announcements on inter-city trains are given in Dutch and French, and text-screen panels in each carriage give the name of the next station. Information and assistance are available at both cities' railway stations.

There are first- and second-class carriages. Smoking is banned on all trains. A range of discounts is offered at weekends and on long-term passes.

V

VISAS AND ENTRY REQUIREMENTS

Visitors from Schengen Zone EU countries only need an identity card to enter Belgium. Visitors from the UK will need to take their passports. Citizens of most other countries including the US, Canada, Australia and New Zealand must have a valid passport. European and North American residents are not subject to any health requirements. In case of doubt, check with Belgian representatives in your own country before departure.

As Belgium is a member of the European Union (EU), free exchange of non-duty-free goods for personal use is permitted between Belgium and the UK and Ireland.

Currency restrictions. There is no limit on the amount of euros or other currency that can be brought into or taken out of the country by non-residents. Sums over €10,000 must be declared when arriving from outside the EU.

WEBSITES

Useful general information can be found at www.visitbelgium.com and www.visitflanders.co.uk. The local tourist boards for both Bruges and Ghent operate easy to navigate websites giving information on hotels, attractions, and more: www.visitbruges.be and www.visitgent. be. Useful sites for planning your travel arrangements are www.belgianrail.be and www.brusselsairport.be. In addition, most hotels have their own websites.

YOUTH HOSTELS

Bruges and its immediate neighbourhood have a number of 'Youth Hotels' and Youth Hostels. There are three located in the city itself, notably: Bauhaus International Youth & Budget Hotel, Langestraat 133-7, 8000 Bruges, tel: 050-34 10 93, www.bauhaus.be

The Passage, Dweersstraat 26, 8000 Bruges, tel: 050-34 02 32, www. passagebruges.com

Snuffel Backpackers Hostel, Ezelstraat 47-9, 8000 Bruges, tel: 050-33 31 33, www.snuffel.be

RECOMMENDED HOTELS

With more than 100 hotels throughout the city, Bruges has a wide range of establishments and locations. Hotels that are part of an international chain will provide a predictable degree of comfort, but guests may miss the more authentic Flemish hospitality offered by locally run establishments. The tourist information office provides brochures listing hotels. It is always advisable to book in advance. Bruges is particularly crowded in the summer, tending to be busiest at weekends. If you trust to luck and arrive with no place to stay, go straight to the tourist office (see page 131), which can almost guarantee to find you something.

Prices are based on the cost per night of a double room with en-suite bath or shower, including service charge, sales tax and breakfast. Rates can vary according to the season or time of the week. All the hotels listed here accept major credit cards.

€€€€	above 300 euros
€€€	200–300 euros
€€	100–200 euros
€	below 100 euros

BRUGES

Acacia €€ *Korte Zilverstraat 3A–5, 8000 Bruges, tel: 050-34 44 11,* www.hotel-acacia.com. This comfortable modern hotel (part of the Best Western chain) is centrally located just off the Markt. All rooms have a private bathroom, television, minibar, telephone and safe; some have air conditioning. Has parking for 20 cars. A continental buffet breakfast is served every morning.

Azalea €€ *Wulfhagestraat 43, 8000 Bruges, tel: 050-33 14 78,* http://azalea.hotel-in-bruges.com. Family-run, this 14th-century house sits on the banks of the Speelmansrei canal, just 200m/yds from the Markt. Comfortably furnished, with a lovely Art Nouveau staircase.

Bauhaus Budget Hotel € *Langestraat 133–7, tel: 050-34 10 93*, www. bauhaus.be. This decent low-cost hotel is close to the eastern ring canal park. Although it might not win many design awards, the rooms ranging in size from singles to quads, and an atmospheric bar-restaurant, are undoubted draws for the youthful clientele that shows up here.

Bourgoensche Cruyce €€ *Wollestraat 41–3, 8000 Bruges, tel: 050-33 79 26*, www.bourgoenschecruyce.be. This is a tiny, charming wooden-fronted hotel (just 16 rooms) in a superb canalside location. Rooms are decorated in sumptuous 17th-century Flemish style with carved antique furniture, stone floors and large fireplaces. The hotel featured in the 2008 hit film *In Bruges*.

Bryghia €€ *Oosterlingenplein 4; tel: 050-33 80 59*; www.bryghiahotel.be. This friendly, family-run hotel is situated in a peaceful neighbourhood, rarely visited by tourists. Part of it occupies a 15th-century building that once belonged to Hanseatic merchants. The interior is cosy and tastefully furnished with comfortable sofas and wood beams. Some rooms enjoy a view of a quiet canal.

Cavalier € *Kuipersstraat 25, 8000 Bruges, tel: 050-33 02 07*, www.hotel cavalier.be. In spite of its slightly ramshackle external appearance, this small hotel (eight rooms) behind the city theatre is friendly and ordered and offers good value in the cheaper range of hotels.

Central € *Markt 30, 8000 Bruges, tel: 050-33 18 05*, www.hotelcentral. be. The name is entirely appropriate, since it would be hard to imagine a more central location in Bruges than on the Markt, directly facing the Belfry. This great-value small hotel has eight smart rooms, and there is a fine restaurant downstairs with a terrace on the square. Breakfast included.

Crowne Plaza Bruges €€€ *Burg 10, 8000 Bruges, tel: 050-44 68 44*, www.ihg.com. Centrally located deluxe hotel that's an intriguing blend of ancient and modern: the building incorporates the foundations of the demolished medieval St Donatian's Cathedral, part of the

10th-century city wall and a 16th-century cellar. Bedrooms are well equipped (some have views of the historic Burg) and there is a pool and wellness centre.

De Orangerie €€€€ *Kartuizerinnenstraat 10, 8000 Bruges, tel: 050-34 16 49, www.hotelorangerie.be.* This luxurious hotel is wonderfully situated on the banks of the canal opposite Dijver. The rooms are all individually furnished, with lavish marble bathrooms. Breakfast on the canalside veranda on a warm summer morning is a real delight.

De Tuilerieen €€€ *Dijver 7, 8000 Bruges, tel: 050-34 36 91, www.hotel tuilerieen.com.* Situated just a few doors away from the main museums, this sumptuous hotel offers has romantic-style rooms, some of which have views of the Dijver canal. Facilities include a pool, sauna, solarium and bar.

Die Swaene €€€ *Steenhouwersdijk 1, 8000 Bruges, tel: 050-34 27 98, www.dieswaene.com.* Award-winning romantic hotel with charming, attentive staff and rooms elegantly and individually furnished to a high standard. The lounge was originally the Guild Hall of the Tailors. Some of the rooms are in a separate wing, called the Canal House.

Duc de Bourgogne €€ *Huidenvettersplein 12, 8000 Bruges, tel: 050-33 20 38, www.ducdebourgogne.be.* This small hotel occupies an attractive step-gabled house in historic Huidenvettersplein (Tanners' Square), right in the heart of the city. The hotel is elegantly, if a little over-ornately, decorated, with lots of tapestries adorning the walls and lavish antique furniture.

Egmond €€ *Minnewater 15, 8000 Bruges, tel: 050-34 14 45, www.egmond. be.* There are just eight rooms in this hotel, which occupies a large 18th-century mansion with its own gardens, beside the Minnewater Park, giving it a tranquil, rural ambience. The rooms are furnished in traditional style and look out over the park.

Fevery € *Collaert Mansionstraat 3, 8000 Bruges, tel: 050-33 12 69, www. hotelfevery.be.* A small, friendly family-run eco-hotel in an extremely quiet location just off Langerei, the long canal that reaches towards the north of the city. Bikes are available for hire.

Graaf van Vlaanderen € *'t Zand 19, 8000 Bruges, tel: 050-33 31 50*, www. graafvanvlaanderen.be. A good budget choice, this small, family-run hotel has pleasant rooms, a bustling restaurant and tearoom, and a lively atmosphere emanating from the nightlife options on its doorstep.

Gulden Vlies €€ *Koningin Elisabethlaan 40, 8000 Brugge, tel: 050-34 12 70*, www.guldenvlies.be. Small family-run hotel with Art Deco touches outside and smart rooms inside. A 15-minute walk north of the centre.

Heritage €€ *Niklaas Desparsstraat 11, 8000 Bruges, tel: 050-44 44 44*, www.hotel-heritage.com. A hotel that delivers country-manor style within an old Bruges town house. The rooms are relatively small, but luxuriously appointed, and the breakfast room has a decorated ceiling with a chandelier. There is an excellent restaurant serving French-Flemish food.

Hotel Navarra Brugge €€€ *Sint-Jakobsstraat 41, 8000 Bruges, tel: 050-34 05 61*, www.hotelnavarra.com. Housed in a mansion that used to be a royal residence in the 17th century – albeit 'only' of a prince – this thoroughly modernised hotel treats its guests like minor royalty. You can relax in the garden and kick back in the wellness centre.

Jan Brito €€ *Freren Fonteinstraat 1, 8000 Bruges, tel: 050-33 06 01*, www. janbrito.eu. Beautifully restored 16th-century mansion, full of period detail, situated just a short walk away from the city's major attractions.

Lucca € *Naaldenstraat 30, 8000 Bruges, tel: 050-34 20 67*, www.hotel lucca.be. Housed in a building that stands atop a 14th-century cellar once used by Italian traders from Lucca, this fine little hotel offers a lot of traditional atmosphere in its breakfast room and other public spaces, and plain character in the rooms.

Martin's Relais Oud Huis Amsterdam €€€€ *Genthof 4A, 8000 Bruges, tel: 050-34 18 10*, www.martins-hotels.com. A rambling canalside building, parts of which date from the 14th century, are the setting for this fine hotel with large, ornate rooms. Those in the front have a canal view and those at the back look out onto a courtyard and garden. There is a wooden staircase, chandeliers and oak beams and a pretty interior courtyard.

Montanus €€ *Nieuwe Gentweg 76–8, 8000 Bruges, tel: 050-33 11 76,* www. montanus.be. Tasteful, restrained elegance in a historic house. In addition to the bedrooms, there are colonial-style pavilion rooms inside the house, and a cedarwood suite in the serene private garden.

NH Brugge €€€ *Boeveriestraat 2, 8000 Bruges, tel: 050-44 97 11,* www. nh-hotels.com. Large rooms and an atmospheric setting in a 17th-century monastery just off the bustling 't Zand Square add character to this large and well-equipped hotel, which has its own heated indoor swimming pool.

Prinsenhof €€€ *Ontvangersstraat 9, 8000 Bruges, tel: 050-34 26 90,* www.prinsenhof.be. This elegant hotel is traditionally furnished, with wood panelling, chandeliers, and antiques; it also has excellent bathrooms. It has a warm atmosphere, and possibly the best breakfast in Bruges.

Rosenburg €€ *Coupure 30, 8000 Bruges, tel: 050-34 01 94,* www. rosenburg.be. A quiet hotel situated on the banks of a canal approximately a 10-minute walk from the centre of Bruges. The atmosphere in this modern brick building is relaxed and friendly, and staff are particularly helpful.

Ter Brughe €€ *Oost-Gistelhof 2, 8000 Bruges, tel: 050-34 03 24,* www. hotelterbrughe.com. Extremely attractive hotel in the elegant St Giles quarter, five minutes' walk from the centre of Bruges. Breakfast is served in the 14th-century beamed and vaulted cellar, which was once a warehouse for goods brought along the canal.

Ter Duinen €€ *Langerei 52, 8000 Bruges, tel: 050-33 04 37,* www.ter duinenhotel.eu. This pleasant waterfront hotel set along the canal stretching northeast from the city centre offers a good compromise between essential facilities and cost, modern fittings and traditional looks.

Ter Reien €€ *Langestraat 1, 8000 Bruges, tel: 050-34 91 00*, www.hotel terreien.be. 'The Canals' hotel is an inexpensive option on the junction of two lovely canals, and occupies the house where the Symbolist painter Fernand Khnopff spent his childhood. All 26 rooms are non-smoking and are bright and comfortable, although some have bathrooms which are rather too small. They face the canal, courtyard or street, and prices reflect this. Breakfast can be taken in the pretty courtyard.

The Pand Hotel €€€ *Pandreitje 16, 8000 Bruges, tel: 050-34 06 66*, www. pandhotel.com. Old-fashioned furnishings complement modern conveniences and lend an authentic touch to the rooms in this quiet hotel set in an 18th-century mansion near the Markt. The excellent breakfasts are cooked on a cast-iron range in the breakfast room.

GHENT

Best Western Residence Hotel Cour St-Georges €€ *Botermarkt 2, 9000 Ghent, tel: 09-224 24 24*, www.courstgeorges.be. Most of the rooms at this hotel are actually in a modern, rather basic annexe situated across the road from the ancient building (originally the house used by the Guild of Crossbowmen), which dates back to 1228.

Flandria Hotel € *Barrestraat 3, 9000 Ghent, tel: 09-223 06 26*, www.flan dria-centrum.be. Cheap, basic 23-room hotel in a quiet side street close to the cathedral. Ideal for those on a shoestring budget looking only for a place to sleep, wash and change their clothes. Substantial breakfasts and friendly staff. Some disabled access.

Ghent River Hotel €€€€ *Waaistraat 5, tel: 09-266 10 10*, www.ghent-river-hotel.be. This stylish waterfront hotel near the Vrijdagmarkt evokes the trading history of Ghent. Some rooms occupy a restored 19th-century sugar factory, while others are in a 16th-century town house; the square was the site of a yarn market in the Middle Ages and the 19th century. When booking, ask for one of the rooms in the former factory, as these have oak beams, brick walls and odd industrial implements used for decoration. The rooms in the modern extension are plainer. The hotel has a rooftop breakfast room with striking views of the old city, a jetty and a fitness room.

Gravensteen €€ *Jan Breydelstraat 35, 9000 Ghent, tel: 09-225 11 50*, www. gravensteen.be. This 19th-century mansion, once the home of an industrial magnate, has been turned into one of the city's most elegant yet friendly hotels. It is situated across the water from the Gravensteen castle, of which the rooms at the front have a fine view, and it has been tastefully renovated and extended. There is a fitness room and sauna.

Hotel Onderbergen €€ *Onderbergen 69, 9000 Ghent, tel: 09-223 62 00*, www.hotelonderbergen.be. Excellent-value boutique hotel a five-minute walk south of the centre. Rooms are spacious and feature hand-painted wallpaper.

Monasterium €€ *Oude Houtlei 56, 9000 Ghent, tel: 09-269 22 10*, www. monasterium.be. This converted 19th-century neo-Gothic convent offers standard modern rooms, as well as some simpler, cheaper rooms (€) in the adjoining Guesthouse PoortAckere. Located in what were formerly nuns' cells, these rooms are fairly basic but ideal for budget travellers. Breakfast (extra charge) is served in an ornate refectory.

NH Gent-Belfort €€€ *Hoogpoort 63, 9000 Ghent, tel: 09-233 33 31*, www. nh-hotels.com. Superbly located opposite the Stadhuis, the Gent-Belfort offers excellent value for a hotel of this quality. The bright, lively rooms are well appointed and extremely comfortable, with splendid bathrooms. One of the two bars is in an historic crypt. There is a fitness room and sauna.

DICTIONARY

adj adjective   **adv** adverb   **BE** British English   **n** noun   **prep** preposition   **v** verb

A

about (approximately) ongeveer; **(regarding)** over
above boven
abroad in het buitenland
accept accepteren
access toegang
accident ongeluk
accidentally per ongeluk
accommodations logies
accompany meegaan
acetaminophen paracetamol
acne acne
across naar de overkant
acupuncture acupunctuur
adapter adapter
additional extra
address adres
adjoining aangrenzend
admission charge toegangsprijs
adult volwassene
after na
afternoon middag
aftershave aftershave
agree akkoord gaan
air lucht
air conditioning airco
air mattress luchtbed
air pump luchtpomp
airmail luchtpost
airport vliegveld
airsickness luchtziekte
aisle gangpad
alarm clock wekker
all alle
allergic allergisch
allergy allergie
alley steegje

all-night pharmacy nachtapotheek
allow toestaan
allowance (quantity) toegestane hoeveelheid; **(permit)** vergunning
almost bijna
alone alleen
already al
also ook
alter vermaken
alternate adj alternatief
aluminum foil aluminiumfolie
always altijd
amazing verbazingwekkend
ambassador ambassadeur
ambulance ambulance
American n Amerikaan; adj Amerikaans
amount (money) bedrag; **(quantity)** hoeveelheid
amusement park pretpark
anesthetic verdovingsmiddel
and en
anemia bloedarmoede
animal dier
another een ander
antacid antacidum
antibiotics antibiotica
antifreeze antivries
antique antiek
antiseptic adj antiseptisch
any wat
anyone iemand
anything iets
apartment appartement
apologize zich verontschuldigen

appendix blindedarm
appetite eetlust
appointment afspraak
approve goedkeuren
approximately ongeveer
arcade speelhal
area code netnummer
arm arm
aromatherapy aromatherapie
around rond
art gallery kunstgalerie
arthritis artritis
ashtray asbak
ask vragen
aspirin aspirine
assistance hulp
asthma astma
at (time) om; **(place)** op
ATM geldautomaat
attack aanval
attractive aantrekkelijk
audio guide audiogids
aunt tante
Australia Australië
authentic authentiek
authenticity echtheid
automatic (car) automaat
available (seat) vrij; **(general)** beschikbaar
away adv weg
awful afschuwelijk

B

baby baby
baby bottle zuigfles
baby food babyvoeding
baby wipes babydoekjes
babysitter oppas

back (body part) rug; **(not front)** achterkant
backache rugpijn
backpack rugzak
bad slecht
bag tas
baggage [BE] bagage
baggage claim bagageafhaalruimte
bake bakken
bakery bakker
balcony balkon
ball bal
ballet ballet
band band
bandage (small) pleister; **(large)** verband
bank bank
bank charges bankkosten
bar bar
barber herenkapper
bargain koopje
barrier barrière
baseball honkbal
basement kelder
basket mand
basketball basketbal
bath bad
bathroom (bath/shower) badkamer; **(restroom)** toilet
battery (general) batterij; **(car)** accu
battlesite slagveld
be zijn
beach strand
beautiful mooi
because omdat
become worden
bed bed
bed and breakfast logies en ontbijt

bedding beddengoed
bedroom slaapkamer
before voor
begin beginnen
beginner beginner
behind achter
Belgium België
belong toebehoren
belt riem
bet wedden
between tussen
beware oppassen
bib slabbetje
bicycle fiets
big groot
bike path fietspad
bikini bikini
bill *n* rekening
binoculars verrekijker
bird vogel
birthday verjaardag
bite (general) beet;
　(insect) beet; *v* bijten
bitter bitter
bizarre bizar
bladder blaas
blanket deken
bleach bleekmiddel
bleed bloeden
blister blaar
blocked (drain) verstopt;
　(road) versperd
blood bloed
blood group bloedgroep
blood pressure
　bloeddruk
blouse bloes
blow dry föhnen
blue blauw
board *v* boarden
boarding pass instapkaart
boat trip boottocht
bone bot
book boek
bookstore boekwinkel
boots laarzen
boring saai
born geboren
borrow lenen
botanical garden
　botanische tuin

bother *v* lastigvallen
bottle fles
bottle opener flesopener
boulevard boulevard
bowel darm
bowl kom
box doos
boxing boksen
boy jongen
boyfriend vriend
bra beha
bracelet armband
brake rem
break *v* breken
break down (car) pech
　hebben; **(appliance)**
　defect raken
breakfast ontbijt
breast borst
breastfeed borst geven
breathe ademhalen
bridge brug
bring brengen
British *n* Britten; *adj* Brits
brochure brochure
broken (body part or
　thing) gebroken;
　(thing) kapot
bronchitis bronchitis
brooch broche
broom bezem
bruise blauwe plek
bucket emmer
bug insect
building gebouw
build *v* bouwen
bulletin board
　mededelingenbord
burn brandwond
bus bus
bus lane busbaan
bus route busroute
bus shelter bushokje
bus station busstation
bus stop bushalte
bus ticket strippenkaart
business zaken
business card
　visitekaartje
business center
　bedrijvencomplex

business class
　businessclass
business district
　zakendistrict
busy druk
but maar
butane gas butagas
butcher slager
button knoop
buy kopen
by (near) bij; **(time)** niet
　later dan
bye (also used at
　arrival) dag; **(only at**
　departure) tot ziens

C

cabin hut
cafe café
calendar kalender
call *n* gesprek; **(phone)**
　v bellen; **(name)**
　v heten
calorie calorie
camera fototoestel
camp *v* kamperen
campsite camping
can (may) mogen;
　(be able) kunnen
can opener blikopener
Canada Canada
canal (general) kanaal;
　(in city) gracht
cancel annuleren
cancer kanker
candle kaars
canoeing kanovaren
cap (hat) pet; **(dental)**
　kroon
capsule (medication)
　capsule
car (vehicle) auto;
　(train compartment)
　wagon
car deck (ferry) autodek
car hire [BE]
　autoverhuurbedrijf
car park [BE]
　parkeerplaats
car rental
　autoverhuurbedrijf

car seat kinderzitje
card kaart
careful voorzichtig
carpet tapijt
carry-on luggage
　handbagage
cart wagentje
carton doos
cash *adv* contant;
　v verzilveren
cash register kassa
casino casino
castle kasteel
catch pakken; **(bus)**
　nemen
cathedral kathedraal
caution oppassen
cave grot
CD cd
CD player cd-speler
cell phone (informal)
　mobiel; **(formal)**
　mobiele telefoon
cemetery begraafplaats
ceramics keramiek
certificate certificaat
change (money)
　n wisselgeld; **(buses)**
　v overstappen;
　(money) *v* wisselen;
　(reservation)
　v veranderen; **(baby)**
　v verschonen
charcoal houtskool
charge *n* prijs;
　v berekenen
cheap goedkoop
check *n* rekening;
　v checken
check in inchecken
check out (hotel)
　uitchecken
checking account
　betaalrekening
cheers proost
chemical toilet
　chemisch toilet
chemist [BE] (with
　prescriptions)
　apotheek; **(without**
　prescriptions)

drogisterij
cheque [BE] rekening
chest borstkas
child kind
child seat kinderstoeltje
child's cot [BE] wieg
children's clothing
kinderkleding
children's menu
kindermenu
children's portion
kinderportie
choose selecteren
church kerk
cigarette sigaret
cigar sigaar
cinema [BE] bioscoop
class klas
clean schoon
cleaning supplies
schoonmaakmiddelen
clearance opruiming
cliff klif
cling film [BE]
huishoudfolie
clinic kliniek
clock klok
clog n klomp
close adv dichtbij;
v sluiten
clothing store
kledingwinkel
cloudy bewolkt
club club
coast kust
coat jas
coat check garderobe
coat hanger kleerhanger
code code
coin munt
cold (chilly) koud; **(flu)**
verkoudheid
collapse instorten
colleague collega
collect ophalen
collection (mail) lichting
color kleur
comb kam
come komen
commission commissie
compact compact

company
(business) bedrijf;
(companionship)
gezelschap
compartment (train)
coupé
computer computer
concert concert
concert hall
concertgebouw
concession concessie
concussion
hersenschudding
conditioner conditioner
condom condoom
conductor dirigent
conference conferentie
confirm bevestigen
congratulations
gefeliciteerd
connect verbinding maken
connection verbinding
conscious bewust
conservation area
beschermd natuurgebied
constant constant
constipation constipatie
consulate consulaat
consult raadplegen
contact bereiken
contact lens contactlens
contact lens solution
contactlensvloeistof
contagious besmettelijk
contain bevatten
contemporary modern
contest wedstrijd
continuous doorlopend
contraceptive
voorbehoedsmiddel
contribution bijdrage
control controle
convention congres
convention hall
congresgebouw
cook n kok; v koken
cooker [BE] fornuis
cooking (cuisine)
keuken
cooking facilities
kookgelegenheid

cool (cold) koel; **(nice)**
cool
copper koper
copy n kopie; v kopiëren
corkscrew kurkentrekker
corner hoek
correct correct
cosmetic cosmetisch
cost kosten
costume (local)
klederdracht
cot ledikant
cottage vakantiehuisje
cotton katoen
cough n hoest; v hoesten
could kunnen
counter (shop) toonbank
country land
country code landnummer
courier koerier
course (meal) gang;
(medication) kuur
courthouse rechtbank
cousin (male) neef;
(female) nicht
cover charge couvert
craft shop
handwerkwinkel
cramps kramp
credit card creditcard
crib wieg
cross n kruis; v oversteken
crossing overtocht
crosswalk zebrapad
crowded vol
crown (dental) kroon
cruise n cruise; v cruisen
crutches krukken
crystal kristal
cup kopje
currency valuta
currency exchange office
geldwisselkantoor
curtain gordijn
curve bocht
custom made op maat
gemaakt
customer information
klanteninformatie
customer service
klantenservice

customs douane
customs declaration
form douaneaangifte-
formulier
cut n snijwond; v knippen
cute schattig
cycle route fietsroute
cycling fietsen
cycling race
wielerwedstrijd

D

daily dagelijks
dairy zuivel
dairy products
zuivelproducten
damage schade
damaged beschadigd
damp vochtig
dance n dans; v dansen
dance club discotheek
dangerous gevaarlijk
dark donker
date of birth
geboortedatum
dawn dageraad
day dag
day trip dagtocht
dead end doodlopende weg
deaf doof
deck chair ligstoel
declare aangeven
decorative decoratief
decorative tile siertegel
deep diep
defrost ontdooien
degree graad
delay vertraging
delete verwijderen
Delft blue Delfts blauw
delicatessen
delicatessen
delicious heerlijk
deliver (give birth)
bevallen; **(bring)**
afleveren
delivery levering
denim spijkerstof
dental floss floss
dental office
tandartspraktijk

dentist tandarts
denture kunstgebit
deodorant deodorant
depart vertrekken
department store
  warenhuis
departure gate
  vertrekgate
departure lounge
  vertrekhal
departures vertrek
deposit n borgsom
describe beschrijven
destination bestemming
detail detail
detergent wasmiddel
detour omleiding
develop ontwikkelen
diabetes diabetes
diabetic adj diabetisch;
  n suikerpatiënt
dial (phone) v kiezen
diamond diamant
diaper luier
diarrhea diarree
diabetic suikerpatiënt
dice dobbelsteen
dictionary woordenboek
diesel diesel
diet dieet
difficult moeilijk
digital digitaal
dine dineren
dining car
  restauratiewagen
dining room eetkamer
dinner avondeten
direct adj rechtstreeks; v
  de weg wijzen
direction richting
directions (map)
  aanwijzingen
directory (phone)
  telefoonboek
dirty vies
disabled gehandicapt
disconnect verbinding
  verbreken
discount korting
discount store
  discountzaak

dish (plate) bord; (food)
  gerecht
dishwasher
  afwasmachine
dishwashing liquid
  afwasmiddel
dislocate ontwrichten
display case vitrine
disposable wegwerpbaar
dissolve oplossen
distance afstand
disturb storen
dive duiken
diving equipment
  duikapparatuur
divorce scheiden
dizzy duizelig
do doen
dock dok
doctor dokter
dog hond
doll pop
dollar (U.S.) dollar
domestic binnenlands
donation gift
door deur
dosage dosering
double dubbel
double room
  tweepersoonskamer
downstairs beneden
downtown stadscentrum
dozen dozijn
dress n jurk; v aankleden
dress code
  kledingvoorschriften
drink n drankje;
  v drinken
drip druppelen
drive rijden
driver chauffeur
driver's license rijbewijs
drop (medicine) druppel
drown verdrinken
drowsy suf
drowsiness sufheid
drugstore drogisterij
drunk dronken
dry droog
dry clean stomen
dry cleaner stomerij

dubbed
  nagesynchroniseerd
dummy [BE] fopspeen
during tijdens
Dutch (language)
  Nederlands; (people)
  Nederlanders
duty (tax) accijns
duty-free belastingvrij

E

ear oor
ear drops oordruppels
earache oorpijn
early vroeg
earrings oorbellen
east oost
easy makkelijk
eat eten
economy class (general)
  economy class; (train)
  tweede klas
electrical outlet
  stopcontact
electronic elektronisch
elevator n lift
e-mail e-mail
e-mail address
  e-mailadres
embassy ambassade
emerald smaragd
emergency noodgeval
emergency brake
  noodrem
emergency exit
  nooduitgang
emergency service
  hulpdienst
empty adj leeg;
  v leegmaken
end n einde; v aflopen
engaged (marriage)
  verloofd
England Engeland
English Engels
English-speaking
  Engelstalig
engrave graveren
enjoy leuk vinden
enlarge vergroten
enough genoeg

entertainment guide
  uitgids
entrance ingang
entrance fee
  toegangsprijs
entrance ramp (highway)
  oprit snelweg
entry ingang
entry visa inreisvisum
envelope envelop
epileptic epileptisch
equipment (clothing)
  uitrusting; (machine)
  apparatuur
error fout
escalator roltrap
essential essentieel
e-ticket e-ticket
euro euro
Eurocheque Eurocheque
evening avond
event evenement
every elk
exact exact
examination onderzoek
example voorbeeld
except uitgezonderd
excess luggage
  overbagage
exchange (general)
  ruilen; (money)
  wisselen
exchange rate
  wisselkoers
excursion excursie
exhausted uitgeput
exit (door) uitgang;
  (highway) afslag
exit ramp afrit
expensive duur
experience ervaring
expiration date
  vervaldatum
expose blootstellen
express mail per expres
extension (phone)
  toestel
extra (additional) extra
extract v onttrekken
eye oog
eyebrow wenkbrauw

F

fabric stof
face gezicht
facial n gezichtsbehandeling
facilities faciliteiten
factor factor
faint adj zwak; v flauwvallen
fall v vallen
family (immediate) gezin; **(relatives)** familie
famous beroemd
fan n ventilator
far ver
far-sighted verziend
farm boerderij
fast (speedy) snel; **(clock)** loopt voor
fast food fastfood
faucet kraan
faulty defect
favorite favoriet
fax fax
fax machine faxapparaat
fax number faxnummer
feature kenmerk
feed voeden
feel voelen
female vrouwelijk
ferry veerboot
fever koorts
few weinig
fiancé verloofde
field weiland
fight n gevecht; v vechten
fill vullen
fill out invullen
fill up opvullen
filling vulling
film (movie) film; **(camera)** fotorolletje
filter filter
find vinden
fine (good) goed; **(well)** prima; **(police)** boete
finger vinger
fire (campfire) kampvuur; **(disaster)** brand
fire alarm brandalarm

fire brigade [BE] brandweer
fire department brandweer
fire door branddeur
fire escape nooduitgang
fire exit brandtrap
fire extinguisher brandblusser
first eerst
first class eerste klas
fishing v vissen
fit passen
fitting room paskamer
fix (repair) repareren
flash flits
flashlight zaklantaarn
flavor smaak
flea market vlooienmarkt
flight vlucht
flight attendant (male) steward; **(female)** stewardess
flight number vluchtnummer
floor (level) verdieping
florist bloemenwinkel
flower bloem
flu griep
flush doorspoelen
fly n vlieg; v vliegen
fog mist
follow volgen
food voedsel
food poisoning voedselvergiftiging
foot voet
footpath [BE] voetpad
football [BE] voetbal
for voor
for sale te koop
foreign buitenlands
forest bos
forget vergeten
fork vork
form n formulier
formal dress avondkleding
formula (baby) flesvoeding
fountain fontein

fracture breuk
frame (glasses) montuur
free (available) vrij
free of charge gratis
freeze bevriezen
freezer diepvriezer
frequent adj vaak
fresh vers
friend vriend
from (general)/van; (destination) uit
front voorkant
frying pan koekenpan
fuel (gas) benzine
full vol
fun plezier
funny grappig
furniture meubels
fuse zekering
fuse box zekeringkast

G

gallery galerie
game (competition) wedstrijd; **(tennis) game; (toy)** spelletje
garage garage
garbage bag vuilniszak
garden tuin
gas (gasoline) benzine
gas station benzinestation
gas tank benzinetank
gate (airport) gate; (general) hek
gauze gaas
gear versnelling
genuine echt
get (receive) krijgen
get off (bus) uitstappen
gift cadeau
gift store cadeauwinkel
girl meisje
girlfriend vriendin
give geven
glass (drinking) glas
glasses (optical) bril
gloves handschoenen
gluten gluten
go gaan
goggles duikbril
gold goud

golf golf
golf club golfstok
golf course golfbaan
good goed
goodbye dag
gram gram
grass gras
great prima
Great Britain Groot-Brittannië
green groen
greengrocer [BE] groenteman
groundcloth grondzeil
groundsheet [BE] grondzeil
group groep
guarantee garantie
guesthouse pension
guide (tour) gids
guide book gids
guide dog geleidehond
guided tour rondleiding
guided walk begeleide wandeling
guitar gitaar
gym fitnessruimte
gynecologist gynaecoloog

H

hair haar
hairbrush borstel
hairdresser dameskapper
halal halal
half n helft; adj halve
hammer hamer
hand hand
hand luggage handbagage
hand washable met de hand wassen
handbag [BE] handtas
handicapped gehandicapt
handicrafts ambachten
handkerchief zakdoek
hanger klerenhanger
hangover kater
happen gebeuren
happy blij
harbor haven
hard (tough) hard; **(difficult)** moeilijk

hardware store ijzerwarenwinkel
hat hoed
have hebben
hay fever hooikoorts
head hoofd
headache hoofdpijn
health gezondheid
health food reformproducten
health food store reformwinkel
health insurance ziektekostenverzekering
hear v horen
hearing aid gehoorapparaat
hearing impaired slechthorend
heart hart
heart attack hartaanval
heart condition hartkwaal
heat verwarming
heating [BE] verwarming
heavy zwaar
height (person) lengte; **(general)** hoogte
hello hallo
helmet helm
help helpen
her haar
here hier
hi hallo
high hoog
highchair kinderstoel
highway snelweg
hiking wandelen
hiking gear wandeluitrusting
hill heuvel
hire huren
historical historisch
hobby hobby
hold (general) vasthouden; **(phone)** aan de lijn blijven
hole gat
holiday [BE] vakantie
home (place) thuis; **(direction)** naar huis
homemade zelfgemaakt

honeymoon huwelijksreis
horn claxon
horse paard
horseback riding paardrijden
horsetrack paardenrenbaan
hospital ziekenhuis
hot heet
hotel hotel
hour uur
house huis
how hoe
how much hoeveel
how many hoeveel
hug omhelzen
hunger honger
hungry hongerig
hunt jagen
hurry n haast; v haasten
hurt n pijn; v pijn hebben
husband man

I

I ik
ibuprofen ibuprofen
ice-cream parlor ijssalon
ice hockey ijshockey
ice skating schaatsen
identification legitimatiebewijs
ill [BE] ziek
illegal illegaal
imitation imitatie
important belangrijk
improve verbeteren
in in
incline helling
include bevatten
indigestion indigestie
indoor pool binnenbad
inexpensive goedkoop
infect ontsteken
infection infectie
inflammation ontsteking
informal informeel
information (general) informatie; **(phone inquiry)** inlichtingen
information desk informatiebalie

injection injectie
injure verwonden
innocent onschuldig
insect insect
insect bite insectenbeet
insect repellent insectenspray
insert (ATM) invoeren
inside binnen
insist aandringen
insomnia slapeloosheid
instant messenger instant messenger
instead of in plaats van
instructions gebruiksaanwijzing
instructor instructeur
insulin insuline
insurance verzekering
insurance card verzekeringsbewijs
insurance certificate [BE] verzekeringsbewijs
insurance claim schadeclaim
interest (hobby) interesse
interference storing
intermission pauze
international internationaal
International Student Card Internationale Studentenkaart
internet internet
internet cafe internetcafé
internet service internetverbinding
interpreter tolk
intersection kruispunt
into naar
introduce (person) voorstellen
invite uitnodigen
iodine jodium
Ireland Ierland
iron n strijkijzer
is is
itch jeuk
item ding
itemized gespecificeerd

J

jacket jasje
jar pot
jaw kaak
jeans spijkerbroek
jet lag jetlag
jet-ski jetski
jeweler juwelier
jewelry sieraden
job baan
join meedoen
joint adj gezamenlijk; n gewricht
joke grap
journey reis

K

keep houden
keep out verboden toegang
key sleutel
key card sleutelkaart
key ring sleutelring
kiddie pool kinderbadje
kidney nier
kilo kilo
kilometer kilometer
kind (pleasant) aardig; **(type)** soort
kiss v kussen
kitchen keuken
knee knie
knife mes
knock kloppen
know kennen
kosher koosjer

L

label label
lace kant
lactose intolerant lactose-intolerant
ladder ladder
lake meer
lamp lamp
land n land; v landen
lane (traffic) rijstrook; **(path)** laantje
language course taalcursus
large groot

last (end) adj laatst;
(previous) adj vorige;
(keep) v meegaan
late (delayed) vertraagd
launderette [BE]
wasserette
laundromat wasserette
laundry service wasserij
laundry facilities
wasmachines
lawyer advocaat
laxative laxerend middel
lead (road) gaan naar
leader (group)
groepsleider
leak lekken
learn leren
leather leer
leave (depart)
vertrekken; (deposit)
betalen; (forget
something) vergeten
left links
left-luggage office [BE]
bagagedepot
leg (body part) been
legal legaal
lend lenen
length lengte
lens lens
lens cap lensdop
less minder
lesson les
let laten
letter brief
level adj gelijk;
n verdieping
library bibliotheek
life leven
life boat reddingsboot
life guard (pool)
badmeester; (beach)
strandmeester
life jacket reddingsvest
lift [BE] lift
light licht
lightbulb gloeilamp
lighthouse vuurtoren
lighter adj lichter;
n aansteker
line lijn

linen linnen
lip lip
lipstick lippenstift
liquor store slijter
liter liter
little klein
live wonen
living room woonkamer
loafers instappers
lobby (theater, hotel) hal
local plaatselijk
lock n slot; v afsluiten
log on inloggen
log off uitloggen
long lang
long-distance bus
touringcar
long-sighted [BE]
verziend
look n stijl; v kijken
loose los
lorry [BE] vrachtauto
lose verliezen
lost (misplaced) verloren;
(direction) verdwaald
lost-and-found gevonden
voorwerpen
lost property office [BE]
gevonden voorwerpen
lottery loterij
loud (general) luid;
(voice) hard
love n liefde; (general)
v dol zijn op; (romantic)
v houden van
low laag
luggage bagage
luggage cart
bagagewagentje
luggage trolley [BE]
bagagewagentje
lump gezwel
lunch lunch
lung long

M

machine washable in de
machine wassen
madam mevrouw
magazine tijdschrift

magnificent magnifiek
mail n post; v posten
mailbox brievenbus
main grootste
make-up make-up
male mannelijk
mall winkelcentrum
mallet houten hamer
man man
manager manager
mandatory verplicht
manicure manicure
many veel
map kaart
market markt
marry trouwen
mascara mascara
mask masker
mass mis
massage massage
matches lucifers
matinee matinee
mattress matras
maybe misschien
meal maaltijd
mean v betekenen
measure meten
measurement afmeting
measuring cup maatbeker
measuring spoon
maatlepel
mechanic monteur
medication medicijn
medicine geneesmiddel
meet ontmoeten
meeting vergadering
meeting room
vergaderruimte
meeting place
ontmoetingsplaats
member lid
memorial gedenkteken
memory card
geheugenkaart
mend (clothes) verstellen
menstrual cramps
menstruatiepijn
menu menukaart
merge (traffic) invoegen
message bericht
metal metaal

microwave (oven)
magnetron
midday [BE] twaalf uur 's
middags
midnight middernacht
migraine migraine
mini-bar minibar
minute minuut
mirror spiegel
missing kwijt
mistake fout
mobile home camper
mobile phone [BE]
(informal) mobiel;
(formal) mobiele
telefoon
moisturizer (cream)
vochtinbrengende crème
money geld
money order postwissel
month maand
mop dweil
moped brommer
more meer
morning ochtend
mosque moskee
mosquito bite muggenbeet
motion sickness
reisziekte
motor motor
motor boat motorboot
motorcycle motorfiets
motorway [BE] snelweg
mountain berg
mountain bike
mountainbike
moustache snor
mouth mond
move (general) bewegen;
(relocate) verhuizen
movie film
movie theater bioscoop
Mr. De heer (Dhr.); meneer
Mrs. Mevrouw (Mevr.)
much veel
mugging beroving
mug mok
muscle spier
museum museum
music muziek
must moeten

N

nail nagel
nail file nagelvijl
nail salon nagelsalon
name naam
napkin servet
nappy [BE] luier
narrow smal
national nationaal
nationality nationaliteit
native inwoner
nature natuur
nature reserve
  natuurreservaat
nature trail natuurpad
nausea misselijkheid
nauseous misselijk
near dichtbij
nearby in de buurt
nearest dichtstbijzijnde
near-sighted bijziend
necessary nodig
neck nek
necklace halsketting
need v nodig hebben
network netwerk
never nooit
new nieuw
New Zealand Nieuw-
  Zeeland
news nieuws
news agent [BE] kiosk
newspaper krant
newsstand kiosk
next volgende
next to naast
nice fijn
night nacht
night club nachtclub
no (denial) nee;
  (prohibition) niet
no parking parkeerverbod
noisy lawaaierig
non-EU citizens niet-EU-
  ingezetenen
non-smoking niet-roken
non-stop non-stop
noon twaalf uur 's
  middags
normal normaal
north noord

nose neus
not niet
nothing niets
notify informeren
now nu
number nummer
nurse verpleegster
nylon nylon

O

o'clock uur
office kantoor
office hours kantooruren
office supplies kantoor-
  benodigdheden
off-licence [BE] slijter
off-peak (ticket) daluren
office kantoor
often vaak
oil olie
OK oké
old oud
on op
once één keer
one-way (traffic)
  eenrichtingverkeer
one-way ticket enkeltje
only slechts
open adj open; (shop)
  v opengaan; (window)
  v opendoen
opening hours [BE]
  openingstijden
opera opera
operation operatie
opposite tegenover
opticien opticien
or of
orally oraal
orchestra orkest
order bestellen
organize organiseren
original origineel
out uit
outdoor adj openlucht
outdoor pool buitenbad
outside buiten
oval ovaal
oven oven
over (more than)
  meer dan

overcharged teveel
  betaald
overheat oververhit
  worden
overlook uitkijkpunt
overnight in één nacht
owe verschuldigd zijn
own adj eigen; v bezitten
owner eigenaar
oxygen zuurstof

P

pacifier fopspeen
pack inpakken
package pakje
paddling pool [BE]
  kinderzwembad
padlock hangslot
pail emmer
pain pijn
paint v verven
painting schilderij
pair paar
pajamas pyjama
palace paleis
palpitations
  hartkloppingen
panorama panorama
pants lange broek
panty hose panty
paper towel keukenpapier
paracetamol [BE]
  paracetamol
paralysis verlamming
parcel [BE] pak
parents ouders
park n park; v parkeren
parking garage
  parkeergarage
parking lot parkeerplaats
parking meter
  parkeermeter
parking ticket parkeerbon
partner partner
part time parttime
party (social) feestje
pass (a place)
  langskomen; (traffic)
  inhalen
passenger passagier
passport paspoort

password wachtwoord
pastry store
  banketbakker
patient adj geduldig;
  n patiënt
pavement [BE] stoep
pay phone telefoonzuil
pay betalen
payment betaling
pearl parel
pedestrian voetganger
pedestrian crossing
  voetgangersover-
  steekplaats
pedestrian zone
  verkeersvrij gebied
pediatrician kinderarts
pedicure pedicure
peg wasknijper
pen pen
penicillin penicilline
per per
performance voorstelling
perhaps misschien
period (general)
  periode; (menstrual)
  menstruatie
person persoon
petite tenger
petrol [BE] benzine
petrol station [BE]
  benzinestation
pewter tin
pharmacy apotheek
phone n telefoon;
  v telefoneren
phone call
  telefoongesprek
phone card telefoonkaart
phone directory
  telefoongids
phone number
  telefoonnummer
photocopy n kopie;
  v kopiëren
photograph foto
photography fotografie
phrase zinsnede
phrase book taalgids
pick up v ophalen
picnic picknick

picnic area picknickplaats
piece stuk
pill pil
pillow kussen
PIN PIN
pipe (smoking) pijp
pizzeria pizzeria
place plaats
plane vliegtuig
plan plan
plaster [BE] pleister
plastic plastic
plastic wrap huishoudfolie
plate bord
platform spoor
platinum platina
play n toneelstuk; v spelen
playground speeltuin
playpen babybox
pleasant prettig
please alstublieft
plug plug
plunger ontstopper
pneumonia longontsteking
poison gif
police politie
police report proces-
verbaal
police station
politiebureau
pollen count
stuifmeelgehalte
polyester polyester
pond vijver
pool zwembad
popular populair
porcelain porselein
port (harbor) haven
porter kruier
portion portie
post [BE] n post;
v versturen
post office postkantoor
postage posttarief
postbox [BE] brievenbus
postcard ansichtkaart
pot pot
pottery aardewerk
pound pond
pound sterling Britse
pond

power (electricity)
stroom
practice praktijk
pregnant zwanger
premium (gas) super
prepaid phone card
prepaidkaart
prescription recept
present n cadeau; v geven
press persen
pretty mooi
price prijs
print afdrukken
prison gevangenis
private particulier
produce store
groentewinkel
profession beroep
problem probleem
prohibited verboden
program programma
pronounce uitspreken
pub pub
public n publiek;
adj openbaar
pull trekken
pump pomp
pure zuiver
purpose doel
purse (handbag) handtas
push duwen
pushchair [BE]
kinderwagen
put neerzetten

Q

quality kwaliteit
quarter kwart
queue [BE] n rij; v in de
rij staan
quick snel
quiet rustig

R

racetrack circuit
racket (tennis) racket
railroad crossing overweg
railway station [BE]
station
rain n regen; v regenen
raincoat regenjas

rape verkrachting
rapids stroomversnelling
rash uitslag
razor scheerapparaat
reach bereiken
reaction reactie
read lezen
ready klaar
real (genuine) echt
receipt (in shop) bon;
(formal) kwitantie
receive ontvangen
reception (desk) receptie
receptionist receptionist
recommend aanbevelen
reduce verminderen
reduction korting
refrigerator koelkast
refund n terugbetaling;
v terugbetalen
region streek
registered mail
aangetekende post
registration form
inschrijfformulier
regular normaal
relationship relatie
reliable betrouwbaar
religion godsdienst
remember (recall)
herinneren; **(not forget)**
onthouden
remove verwijderen
renovation renovatie
rent n huur; v huren
rental car huurauto
repair repareren
repeat herhalen
replace vervangen
replacement part
vervangingsonderdeel
report n rapport; v melden
required vereist
reservation reservering
reservation desk
reserveringsbalie
reserve reserveren
reservoir reservoir
responsibility
verantwoordelijkheid
rest rusten

rest area rustgebied
restaurant restaurant
restroom toilet
retired gepensioneerd
return ticket [BE]
retourtje
right (correct) juist;
(direction) rechts
ring ring
river rivier
road weg
road map wegenkaart
roadwork
wegwerkzaamheden
rob beroven
robbery beroving
rock rots
romantic romantisch
roof dak
room kamer
room service roomservice
rope touw
rose roos
round rond
round-trip ticket retourtje
route route
row roeien
rowboat roeiboot
rubbish [BE] vuilnis
rude onbeleefd
ruins ruïne
rush haasten

S

safe adj veilig; n kluis
safety veiligheid
safety pin
veiligheidsspeld
sale opruiming
sales tax BTW
same hetzelfde
sand zand
sandals sandalen
sanitary napkin
maandverband
sanitary pad [BE]
maandverband
satin satijn
saucepan steelpan
sauna sauna
save (computer) opslaan

savings account spaarrekening
say zeggen
scarf sjaal
scissors schaar
Scotland Schotland
screwdriver schroevendraaier
sea zee
seasick zeeziek
season ticket abonnement
seat (on train, etc.) plaats
seat belt veiligheidsgordel
sedative kalmerend middel
see zien
self-service zelfbediening
sell verkopen
seminar seminar
send versturen
senior citizen oudere
separated uit elkaar
separate apart
serious ernstig
serve opdienen
service (church) kerkdienst; **(restaurant)** bediening
service charge bedieningsgeld
service included bediening inbegrepen
set menu dagmenu
sew naaien
sex seks
shadow schaduw
shallow ondiep
shampoo shampoo
shape vorm
share delen
sharp scherp
shave scheren
shaving brush scheerkwast
shaving cream scheerzeep
sheet (bed) laken
ship schip

shirt (men's) overhemd
shock schok
shoe schoen
shoe repair schoenmaker
shoe store schoenenwinkel
shop assistant winkelbediende
shopping n boodschappen; v winkelen
shopping basket winkelmandje
shopping centre [BE] winkelcentrum
shopping mall winkelcentrum
shopping cart winkelwagentje
shopping trolley [BE] winkelwagentje
short kort
short-sighted [BE] bijziend
shorts korte broek
shoulder schouder
shovel schep
show tonen
shower douche
shut v sluiten
shutter luik
sick (general) ziek; **(nauseous)** misselijk
side effect bijwerking
sidewalk stoep
sight (attraction) bezienswaardigheid
sightseeing tour toeristische rondrit
sign (road) n verkeersbord; **(place signature)** v tekenen
silk zijde
silver zilver
single (person) single
single ticket [BE] (travel) enkeltje
single room eenpersoonskamer
sink (bathroom) wastafel; **(kitchen)** gootsteen

sit zitten
site plaats
size maat
skating rink ijsbaan
skin huid
skirt rok
sleep slapen
sleeping bag slaapzak
sleeping car slaapwagen
sleeping pill slaappil
sleeve mouw
slice plak
slippers pantoffels
slow langzaam
small klein
smell geur
smoke roken
smoking area rokerszone
snack snack
snack bar snackbar
sneakers gymschoenen
snorkle snorkelen
snow n sneeuw; v sneeuwen
soap zeep
soccer voetbal
socket stopcontact
socks sokken
sold out uitverkocht
some enkele
someone iemand
something iets
sometimes soms
somewhere ergens
soon gauw
soother [BE] fopspeen
sore pijnlijk
sore throat keelpijn
sorry sorry
south zuid
souvenir souvenir
souvenir guide souvenirgids
souvenir store souvenirwinkel
spa kuuroord
space ruimte
spare extra
spatula spatel
speak spreken
special speciaal

specialist specialist
specimen monster
speed snelheid
speed limit snelheidslimiet
spell v spellen
spend uitgeven
sponge spons
spoon lepel
sport sport
sporting goods store sportwinkel
sports club sportvereniging
spot (place, site) plaats
spouse (male) echtgenoot; **(female)** echtgenote
sprain n verstuiking; v verstuiken
square vierkant
stadium stadion
staff personeel
stainless steel roestvrij staal
stairs trap
stamp n postzegel; v stempelen
stand staan
standard standaard
standby ticket standby-ticket
start (general) beginnen; **(car, etc.)** starten
statue standbeeld
stay n verblijf; **(remain)** v blijven; **(overnight)** v logeren
steal stelen
steel staal
steep steil
sterilizing solution steriele oplossing
sterling silver sterling zilver
stiff stijf
still nog
stolen gestolen
stomach maag
stomachache maagpijn
stop n halte; v stoppen

store winkel
store directory [BE]
 winkelplattegrond
store guide
 winkelplattegrond
stove fornuis
straight recht
stream beekje
street straat
stroller kinderwagen
strong sterk
student student
study studeren
stunning verbluffend
style n stijl; v stylen
subtitled ondertiteld
suburb buitenwijk
subway metro
subway map metrokaart
subway station
 metrostation
suggest voorstellen
suit pak
suitable geschikt
suitcase koffer
sun zon
sunbathe zonnebaden
sunblock sunblock
sunburn zonnebrand
sunglasses zonnebril
sunshade [BE] parasol
sunscreen
 zonnebrandcrème
suntan lotion
 zonnebrandcrème
super (petrol) [BE] super
superb voortreffelijk
supermarket supermarkt
supervision toezicht
suppository zetpil
surcharge toeslag
sure zeker
surfboard surfplank
swallow doorslikken
sweater trui
sweatshirt sweatshirt
sweep vegen
sweet zoet
swelling zwelling
swim zwemmen
swimsuit zwempak

swimming pool zwembad
swimming trunks
 zwembroek
swollen opgezet
symbol symbool
symptom symptoom
synagogue synagoge
synthetic synthetisch

T

T-shirt T-shirt
TV tv
table tafel
tablet tablet
take (general) nemen;
 (carry) meenemen;
 (medicine) innemen;
 (time) duren
take off (plane) opstijgen;
 (shoes) uitdoen
talk praten
tall lang
tampon tampon
tap [BE] kraan
taste n smaak; v proeven
taxi taxi
taxi rank [BE]
 taxistandplaats
taxi stand taxistandplaats
teaspoon theelepel
team team
tear (muscle) scheuren
tear off afscheuren
telephone n telefoon;
 v telefoneren
telephone booth
 telefoonzuil
telephone call
 telefoongesprek
telephone number
 telefoonnummer
tell vertellen
temperature temperatuur
tennis tennis
tennis court tennisbaan
tent tent
tent peg tentharing
tent pole tentstok
terminal terminal
terrible vreselijk
text n tekst

text messaging sms'en
thank danken
that dat
theater theater
theft diefstal
then (time) dan
there daar
thermometer
 thermometer
thermos thermosfles
these deze
thick dik
thief dief
thigh dij
thin dun
thing ding
think denken
thirsty dorstig
this dit
those die
throat keel
through door
thumb duim
ticket kaartje
ticket inspector
 conducteur
ticket office loket
tie n stropdas
tight krap
tile tegel
time tijd
timetable [BE]
 dienstregeling
tip fooi
tire band
tired moe
tissue tissue
to (place) naar
tobacco tabak
tobacconist
 sigarenwinkel
today vandaag
toe teen
toilet [BE] toilet
toilet paper toiletpapier
toll tol
toll booth tolhuisje
toll road tolweg
tomorrow morgen
tongue tong
tonight vanavond

too te
tooth tand
toothache kiespijn
toothbrush tandenborstel
toothpaste tandpasta
top bovenkant
torn gescheurd
tour excursie
tour guide reisgids
tourist toerist
tourist office VVV-
 kantoor
tournament toernooi
tow truck takelwagen
towel handdoek
tower toren
town stad
town hall stadhuis
town map
 stadsplattegrond
town square stadsplein
toy speelgoed
toy store
 speelgoedwinkel
traditional traditioneel
traffic verkeer
traffic circle rotonde
traffic jam file
traffic light stoplicht
traffic offence [BE]
 verkeersovertreding
traffic violation
 verkeersovertreding
trail wandelpad
trailer aanhangwagen
train trein
train station station
tram tram
transfer overstappen
transport vervoer
translate vertalen
translation vertaling
translator vertaler
trash vuilnis
trash can vuilnisbak
travel reizen
travel agency reisbureau
travel sickness
 reisziekte
traveler's check
 reischeque

traveller's cheque [BE] reischeque
tray plateau
treatment behandeling
tree boom
trim bijknippen
trip reis
trolley wagentje
trousers [BE] lange broek
truck vrachtwagen
true waar
try on (clothes) passen
tumor tumor
tunnel tunnel
turn (traffic) keren
turn down (volume, heat) lager zetten
turn off uitzetten
turn on aanzetten
turn up hoger zetten
tweezers pincet
twist (ankle) verstuiken
typical typisch

U

U.K. Groot-Brittannië
U.S. Verenigde Staten
ugly lelijk
ulcer zweer
umbrella paraplu
unconscious bewusteloos
under onder
underground station [BE] metrostation
understand begrijpen
unemployed werkeloos
units (phone card) eenheden
until tot
upstairs boven
urgent dringend
use n gebruik; v gebruiken
username gebruikersnaam

V

vacant vrij
vacation vakantie
vacuum cleaner stofzuiger

valet service parkeerdienst
valid geldig
validate (general) bevestigen; **(ticket)** afstempelen
valuable waardevol
value waarde
VAT [BE] BTW
vegan veganist
vegetarian n vegetariër; adj vegetarisch
vehicle voertuig
vein ader
version versie
very heel
video game videospelletje
view uitzicht
viewpoint uitkijkpunt
village dorp
vineyard wijngaard
visa visum
visit n bezoek; v bezoeken
visiting hours bezoekuur
visually impaired slechtziend
volleyball volleybal
voltage voltage
vomit n braaksel; v overgeven

W

wait wachten
waiting room wachtkamer
waiter kelner
waitress kelnerin
wake (self) wakker worden; **(someone)** wakker maken
wake-up service wekdienst
Wales Wales
walk (general) lopen; **(on trail/path)** wandelen
wall muur
wallet portemonnee
ward (hospital) afdeling
warm adj warm; v opwarmen

war memorial oorlogsmonument
warning waarschuwing
washable wasbaar
washing machine wasmachine
watch (timepiece) horloge
water water
water skis waterski's
waterfall waterval
waterproof waterdicht
wave golf
way weg
wear dragen
weather weer
weather forecast weerbericht
wedding huwelijk
week week
weekday weekdag
weekend weekend
weekend rate weekendtarief
weekly wekelijks
weigh wegen
weight gewicht
welcome welkom
west west
wetsuit duikerspak
what wat
wheelchair rolstoel
wheelchair ramp rolstoelopgang
when wanneer
where waar
which welke
while terwijl
who wie
whose van wie
why waarom
wide breed
wife vrouw
wildlife dieren in het wild
wind wind
windbreaker windjack
windmill molen
windscreen voorruit
windsurfing windsurfen
windy winderig

window (general) raam; **(shop)** etalage
window seat plaats bij het raam
wine wijn
wine list wijnkaart
wipe vegen
wireless draadloos
wish wens
with met
withdraw (money) opnemen
withdrawal (money) geldopname
within (time) binnen
without zonder
witness getuige
wood (forest) bos; **(material)** hout
wool wol
work (function) n werk v werken; **(operate)** bedienen
wrap v inpakken
write schrijven
wrong verkeerd

X

x-ray röntgenfoto

Y

yacht jacht
year jaar
yes ja
yesterday gisteren
yield (traffic) voorrang verlenen
you (sing. for.) u; **(sing. inf.)** jij; **(pl. for.)** u; **(pl. inf.)** jullie
young jong
youth jongeren
youth hostel jeugdherberg

Z

zebra crossing [BE] zebrapad
zero nul
zipper ritssluiting
zoo dierentuin

Dutch – English

A

aanbevelen recommend
aandringen insist
aangetekend registered (mail)
aangeven declare
aankleden v dress
aankomst arrivals
aansteker n lighter
aantrekkelijk attractive
aanvaarden accept
aanval attack
aanvang start
aanwijzen indicate
aanwijzingen directions (map)
aanzetten turn on
aardewerk pottery
aardig pleasant
accepteren accept
accijns duty
accu battery
achter behind
achterkant back (opposite of front)
acupunctuur acupuncture
adapter adapter
ademhalen breathe
ader vein
adres address
advocaat lawyer
afdeling department (general); ward (hospital)
afdrukken print
afhalen to go (food) [take away BE]
afleveren deliver (bring)
aflopen v end
afmeting measurement
afrit exit ramp
afschuwelijk awful
afslag highway [motorway BE] exit
afsluiten v lock
afspraak appointment
afstand distance

afstempelen validate
aftershave aftershave
afval trash [rubbish BE]
afwasmachine dishwasher
airco air conditioning
akkoord gaan agree
al already
alle all
alleen only (merely); alone (without company)
allergie allergy
allergisch allergic
alstublieft (a.u.b.) please
alternatief alternative
altijd always
aluminiumfolie aluminum [kitchen BE] foil
ambachten handicrafts
ambassade embassy
ambassadeur ambassador
ambulance ambulance
Amerikaan n American
Amerikaans adj American
andere other
annuleren cancel
ansichtkaart post card
antacidum antacid
antibiotica antibiotics
antiek antique
antiseptisch adj antiseptic
antivries antifreeze
annuleren cancel
apart separate
apparatuur equipment
appartement apartment
apotheek pharmacy [chemist BE]
arm arm
armband bracelet
aromatherapie aromatherapy
arriveren arrive
artritis arthritis

asbak ashtray
aspirine aspirin
assistentie assistance
astma asthma
atletiek athletics
audiogids audio guide
Australië Australia
authentiek authentic
auto car
autodek car deck (ferry)
autosnelweg highway [motorway BE]
autoverhuur car rental [car hire BE]
avond evening
avondeten dinner
avondkleding formal wear

B

baan job
baby baby
babybox playpen
babydoekjes baby wipes
babyvoeding baby food
bad bath
badkamer bathroom
badmeester life guard (pool)
bagageafhaalruimte baggage claim
bagagedepot luggage [baggage BE] check
bagage luggage [baggage BE]
bagagekluisjes luggage lockers
bagagewagentje luggage cart [baggage trolley BE]
bakkerij bakery
bal ball
balkon balcony
ballet ballet
band band
bank bank
banketbakker pastry shop
bar bar

basketbal basketball
batterij battery
bed bed
beddengoed bedding
bedienen work (operate)
bediening service
bediening inbegrepen service included
bedieningsgeld service charge
bedrag amount
bedrijf company (business)
bedrijvencomplex business center
beekje stream
been leg
beet bite
beginnen v begin
beginner beginner
begraafplaats cemetery
begrijpen understand
beha bra
behalve except
behandeling treatment
belangrijk important
belastingvrij duty free
België Belgium
bellen call
benzine gas [petrol BE]
benzinestation gas [petrol BE] station
benzinetank gas tank
bereiken reach
berg mountain
bericht message
beroemd famous
beroep profession
beroven rob
beschikbaar available
beschrijven describe
besmettelijk contagious
bestellen v order
bestemming destination
bestuurder driver
betalen pay
betaling payment
betekenen v mean

betrouwbaar reliable
bevatten contain
bevestigen confirm
bevriezen freeze
bevroren frozen
bewaren keep
bewegen move
bewust conscious
bewusteloos
unconscious
bezem broom
bezet taken
bezienswaardigheid
sight (attraction)
bezitten *v* own
bezoek *n* visit
bezoeken *v* visit
bezoekuur visiting hours
bibliotheek library
bijgewerkt updated
bijknippen *v* trim
bijna almost
bijten bite
bijziend near-sighted
[short-sighted BE]
bikini bikini
binnen inside
binnenbad indoor pool
binnenkomen enter
binnenkomst entrance
binnenlands domestic
bioscoop movie theater
[cinema BE]
bitter bitter
bizar bizarre
blaar blister
blaas bladder
bladeren browse
blauwe plek bruise
bleekmiddel bleach
blij happy
blijven stay
blikopener can opener
blind blind
blindedarm appendix
bloed blood
bloedarmoede anemia
bloeddruk blood pressure
bloedgroep blood group
bloeden bleed
bloem flower

bloemenwinkel flower
shop
bloemist florist
bloes blouse
blokkeren *v* block
blootstellen expose
boarden boarding
(airport)
boardingkaart boarding
card
bocht curve
boek book
boekwinkel bookstore
boerderij farm
boete fine (police)
boksen boxing
bon receipt
boodschappen
n shopping
boom tree
boottocht boat trip
bord plate
borgsom deposit
borst breast
borst geven breastfeed
borstel hairbrush
borstkas chest
bos forest
bot bone
botanische tuin
botanical garden
bouwen build
boven above
bovenkant top
braaksel *n* vomit
brand *n* fire
brandalarm fire alarm
brandblusser fire
extinguisher
branddeur fire door
brandstof fuel
brandtrap fire exit
brandweer fire department [brigade BE]
brandweerkazerne fire
station
brandwond burn
breed wide
breken *v* break
breuk fracture
brief letter

brievenbus mailbox
[postbox BE]
bril glasses (optical)
Brit *n* British
Brits *adj* British
Britse pond pound
sterling
broche brooch
brochure brochure
broer brother
brommer moped
brug bridge
bruin brown
bruinen *v* tan
buiten outside
buitenbad outdoor pool
buitenlands foreign
buitenlijn outside line
(phone)
buiten werking out
of order
buitenwijk suburb
bus bus
busbaan bus lane
bushalte bus stop
bushokje bus shelter
business class
businessclass
busroute bus route
busstation bus station
butagas butane gas

C

cadeau gift
cadeauwinkel gift store
café cafe
calorie calorie
camper mobile home
camping campsite
Canada Canada
capsule capsule
(medication)
casino casino
cd CD
cd-speler CD player
certificaat certificate
chauffeur driver
check-in balie check-in
desk (airport)
chemisch toilet
chemical toilet

circuit racetrack
claxon horn
club club
code code
collect call collect call
[reversed charges BE]
collega colleague
commissie commission
compact compact
computer computer
concert concert
concertgebouw concert
hall
concessie concession
conciërge concierge
conditioner conditioner
condoom condom
conducteur ticket
inspector
conferentie conference
conferentiezaal
conference room
congres convention
congresgebouw
convention hall
constant constant
constipatie constipation
consulaat consulate
contactlens contact
lens
contactlensvloeistof
contact lens solution
contant cash
controle *n* control
cosmetisch cosmetic
coupé compartment
(train)
couvert cover charge
creditcard credit card
cruise *n* cruise
cruisen *v* cruise

D

daar there
dag day (time period);
hello; goodbye
dagelijks daily
dak roof
dames women's restroom
dameskapper
hairdresser

dameskleding ladieswear
dan then (time)
danken n thank
dans n dance
dansen v dance
dat that
decoratief decorative
defect faulty
deken blanket
delen v share
Delfts blauw Delft blue
delicatessen delicatessen
denken think
deodorant deodorant
deposito deposit
detail detail
deur door
De heer (Dhr.) Mr.
de weg wijzen v direct
diamant diamond
diarree diarrhea
dichtbij near
dieet diet
dief thief
diefstal theft
dienblad tray
dienst n service
diep deep
diepvriezer freezer
dier animal
dierentuin zoo
diesel diesel
digitaal digital
dij thigh
dik thick
dineren dine
ding thing
directeur director
dirigent conductor
discotheek dance club
discountzaak discount store
dobbelsteen dice
doel purpose
dok dock
dokter doctor
donker dark
doodlopende weg dead end

doof deaf
dood dead
door through (movement); by (by means of)
doorgaand verkeer through traffic
doorlopend continuous
doorslikken swallow
doorspoelen v flush
doos box
dorp village
dorstig thirsty
dosering dosage
douane customs
douaneaangifteformulier customs declaration form
douanecontrole customs control
douche shower
dozijn dozen
draadloos wireless
draaien v turn (general); play (movie)
dragen wear (clothes)
drankje n drink
dringend urgent
drinken v drink
drogist drugstore [chemist BE]
dronken drunk
droog dry
druk busy
drukken press (clothing)
druppel drop (medication)
druppelen drip
duikbril goggles
duiken v dive
duikerspak wetsuit
duim thumb
duizelig dizzy
dun thin
duren v take (time)
duur expensive
duwen push
dweil mop

E

echt real
echtgenoot spouse (male)
echtgenote spouse (female)

echtheid authenticity
eenheden units (phone card)
eenpersoonskamer single room
eenrichtingsstraat one-way street
eenrichtingsverkeer one-way (traffic)
eerst first
eerste klas first class
eerstehulp (EHBO) first aid
eetkamer dining room
eetlust appetite
eigen adj own
eigendom property
einde n end
elektrisch electric
elektronisch electronic
elk every
e-mail e-mail
e-mailadres e-mail address
en and
Engeland England
Engels English
enkeltje one-way (single BE) ticket
envelop envelope
epileptisch epileptic
ergens somewhere
ernstig serious
ervaring experience
essentieel essential
eten eat
e-ticket e-ticket
euro euro
Eurocheque Eurocheque
even briefly
evenement event
exact exact
excursie tour
expres express
extra adj additional

F

faciliteiten facilities
factor factor
familie family
fastfood fast food

favoriet favorite
fax fax
faxapparaat fax machine
faxnummer fax number
feestdag holiday
feestje party (social)
fiets bicycle
fietspad bicycle path
fietsen cycling
fietsroute bicycle route
fijn nice
file traffic jam
film film (camera); movie [film BE]
filter filter
fitnessruimte gym
flat apartment [flat BE]
flauwvallen v faint
fles bottle
flesopener bottle opener
flesvoeding formula (baby)
flits flash
floss dental floss
föhn hair dryer
fontein fountain
fooi tip
fopspeen pacifier [soother BE]
formulier form
fornuis stove
foto photograph
fotografie photography
fotorolletje film
fototoestel camera
fout mistake

G

gaan go
gaas gauze
galerie gallery
gang hallway (building); course (meal)
gangpad aisle
garage garage
garantie guarantee
garderobe coat check
gat hole
gate gate (airport)
gauw soon
gay club gay club

gebeuren happen
geboortedatum date of birth
geboren born
gebouw building
gebroken broken
gebruik *n* use
gebruiken *v* use
gebruikersnaam username
gebruiksaanwijzing instructions
gedenkteken memorial
geduldig adj patient
geel yellow
geen no
gefeliciteerd congratulations
gehandicapt disabled
geheugenkaart memory card
gehoorapparaat hearing aid
gekoeld refrigerated
geld money
geldautomaat ATM
geldopname withdrawal (money)
geldwisselkantoor currency exchange
geleden ago
geleidehond guide dog
gelijk adv level
gelukkig fortunately
genoeg enough
geopend open
gepensioneerd retired
geschenk gift
geschikt voor de magnetron microwaveable
geschikt suitable
getuige witness
geur smell
gevaarlijk dangerous
gevecht *n* fight
geven give
gevonden voorwerpen lost and found [lost property office BE]

gevorderd advanced
gewicht weight
gewricht *n* joint
gezelschap company (companionship)
gezicht face
gezichtsbehandeling *n* facial
gezin family (immediate)
gezondheid health
gezwel lump
gids guide (tour, book)
gif poison
gift donation
gisteren yesterday
gitaar guitar
glad icy
glas glass (drinking)
gloeilamp light bulb
gluten gluten
godsdienst religion
goed adj good
goederen freight
goedkeuren approve
goedkoop cheap
golf golf (game); wave (water)
golfbaan golf course
golfstok golf club
gootsteen sink
gordijn curtain
goud gold
graad degree
gram gram
grap joke
grappig funny
gras grass
grasduinen browse
gratis free of charge
graveren engrave
griep flu
groentewinkel produce store [greengrocer BE]
groep group
grondzeil groundcloth [groundsheet BE]
groot large
Groot-Brittannië Great Britain
grot cave

gymschoenen sneakers
gynaecoloog gynecologist

H

haar hair
haarspray hairspray
haast *n* rush
haasten *v* rush
hal hall (general); lobby (theater, hotel)
halal halal
hallo hello
half half
halsketting necklace
halte stop (bus, tram)
hamer hammer
hand hand
handbagage carry-on [hand BE] luggage
handdoek towel
handschoenen gloves
handtas purse [handbag BE]
handwerkwinkel craft shop
hangslot padlock
hard hard
hart heart
hartaanval heart attack
hartkloppingen palpitations
hartkwaal heart condition
haven harbor
hebben have
heel very
heerlijk lovely
heet hot
hek gate
helft *n* half
helling incline
helm helmet
helpen help
herenkapper barber
herenkleding menswear
herentoilet men's restroom
herhalen repeat
herinneren remember
hersenschudding concussion

hetzelfde same
heuvel hill
hier here
hij he
historisch historical
hobby hobby
hoe how
hoed hat
hoek corner
hoest *n* cough
hoesten *v* cough
hoeveel how much; how many
hoeveelheid amount
hoger zetten turn up
hond dog
honger hunger
hongerig hungry
honkbal baseball
hoofd head
hoofdpijn headache
hoofdweg main road
hoogte height
hooikoorts hay fever
horen hear
horloge watch
hotel hotel
houden keep
houden van *v* love
hout wood
houten hamer mallet
houtskool charcoal
huid skin
huis house
huishoudfolie plastic wrap [cling film BE]
hulp assistance
hulpdienst emergency service
huren rent
hut cabin
huurauto rental car
huwelijk wedding
huwelijksreis honeymoon

I

iemand someone
Ierland Ireland
iets something
ijsbaan skating rink

ijssalon ice-cream parlor
ijshockey ice hockey
ijzerwarenwinkel hardware store
ik I
illegaal illegal
imitatie imitation
in in
inbegrepen included (price)
ibuprofen ibuprofen
incheckbalie check-in desk
inchecken check-in
indigestie indigestion
infectie infection
informeel informal
informeren notify
informatie information
informatiebalie information desk
informatiebureau information office
ingang entrance
inhalen overtake
inhaalverbod no-passing zone
injectie injection
inloggen log on
innemen take (medication)
inpakken pack (suitcase); wrap (present)
inreisvisum entry visa
inrijden enter (traffic)
insectenbeet insect bite
insectenspray insect repellent
inslaan break
instant messenger instant messenger
instappers loafers
instorten collapse
instructeur instructor
insuline insulin
intensive care intensive care
interessant interesting
interesse interest (hobby)
internationaal international

Internationale Studentenkaart International Student Card
internet internet
internetcafé internet cafe
internetverbinding internet service
intoetsen enter
invullen fill out
invoegen merge (traffic)
invoeren insert
inwendig internally
inwerpen insert
inwoner resident
inwoners van de EU EU citizens

J

ja yes
jaar year
jaar oud aged
jacht yacht
jagen hunt
jas coat
jasje jacket
jazz jazz
jetlag jet lag
jetski jet-ski
jeugdherberg youth hostel
jeuk n itch
jij you (informal)
jodium iodine
jong young
jongen boy
jongeren youth
juist correct
jurk n dress
juwelier jeweler

K

kaak jaw
kaars candle
kaart card (credit card); map (directions)
kaartje ticket
kakkerlak cockroach
kalender calendar
kalmerend middel sedative
kam comb

kamer room
kamermeisje maid (hotel)
kamertarief room rate
kamperen v camp
kampvuur fire
kan jug
kanaal canal
kanker cancer
kanovaren canoeing
kant lace
kantoor office
kantoorbenodigdheden office supplies
kapot broken
kapper barber; hairdresser
kapsel hair cut
karaf carafe
kassa checkout; cash register
kassajuffrouw cashier
kasteel castle
kater hangover
kathedraal cathedral
keel throat
katoen cotton
keelpijn sore throat
keer time
kelder basement
kelner waiter
kelnerin waitress
kenmerk feature
kennen know
keramiek ceramics
kerk church
kerkdienst n service
ketel kettle
ketting chain
keuken kitchen
keukenpapier paper towel
kies v dial (phone)
kiespijn toothache
kijken v look
kilo kilo
kilometer kilometer
kind child
kinderarts pediatrician
kinderkleding children's clothing

kindermenu children's menu
kinderportie children's portion
kinderstoel highchair
kinderwagen stroller (pushchair BE)
kinderzitje car seat
kinderzwembad kiddie (paddling BE) pool
kiosk newsstand (news agent BE)
klaar ready
klanteninformatie customer information
klantenservice customer service
klas class
klederdracht costume (local)
kledingwinkel clothing store
klerenhanger coat hanger
klein small
klem clamp
kleur color
klier gland
klif cliff
kliniek clinic
klok clock
klomp n clog
klooster monastery
kloppen knock
kluis safe
knie knee
knippen v cut
knoop button
koekenpan frying pan
koel cool (temperature)
koelkast refrigerator
koerier courier
koffer suitcase
kok n cook
kom bowl
komen come
kookgelegenheid cooking facilities
koopje bargain
koorts fever
kopen buy

koper copper
kopie n photocopy
kopieerapparaat photocopier
kopiëren v photocopy
kopje cup
kort short
korte broek shorts
korting discount
koosjer kosher
kosten v cost
koud adj cold
kousen stockings
kraan faucet [tap BE]
kraanwater tap water
kramp cramps
krant newspaper
krap tight
krijgen get (receive)
kristal crystal
kroon crown (dental)
kruidenierswinkel grocery store [greengrocer BE]
kruier porter
kruis n cross
kruispunt intersection [junction BE]
krukken crutches
kwitantie receipt
kuil pothole (road)
kunnen v can
kunstenaar artist
kunstgalerie art gallery
kunstgebit denture
kurkentrekker corkscrew
kussen n pillow; v kiss
kust coast
kuuroord spa
kwaliteit quality
kwart quarter
kwijt missing

L

laag low
laantje lane
laarzen boots
laat late
laatste last
label label

lactose-intolerant lactose intolerant
ladder ladder
lager zetten turn down (volume, heat)
laken sheet
lamp lamp
land country
landen v land
landnummer country code
lang long
lange broek pants [trousers BE]
langzaam slow
laten zien show
lawaaierig noisy
laxerend middel laxative
ledikant cot
leeg adj empty (general); dead (battery)
leegmaken v empty
leer leather
legaal legal
legitimatiebewijs ID
lekken v leak
lekker delicious
lelijk ugly
lenen borrow (from); lend (to)
lengte height (person); length (general)
lens lens
lensdop lens cap
lepel spoon
leren learn
les lesson
leuk vinden enjoy
leunen lean
leven life
lever liver
levering delivery
lezen read
licht light
lichten headlights (car)
lichting collection (mail)
lid member
liefde n love
lift elevator [lift BE]
ligstoel deck chair
lijn line

limousine limousine
links left
linnen linen
lip lip
lippenstift lipstick
liter liter
logeren stay (overnight)
logies accommodations
logies-ontbijt bed and breakfast
lokaal local
loket ticket office
long lung
longontsteking pneumonia
loodvrij unleaded (gasoline)
lopen v walk
los loose
losschroeven unscrew
loterij lottery
lucht air
luchtbed air mattress
luchtpomp air pump
luchtpost airmail
luchtvaartmaatschappij airline
luchtziekte airsickness
lucifers matches
luid loud
luier diaper [nappy BE]
luik shutter
lunch lunch

M

maag stomach
maagpijn stomachache
maaltijd meal
maand month
maandverband sanitary napkin [pad BE]
maar but
maat size
maatbeker measuring cup
maatlepel measuring spoon
machine machine
magnetron microwave (oven)
magnifiek magnificent

maken make
make-up make-up
makkelijk easy
man man; husband
manager manager
mand basket
manicure manicure
mannelijk male
markt market
mascara mascara
masker mask
massage massage
matinee matinee
matras mattress
mededelingenbord bulletin board
medicijn medication
medische nooddienst emergency medical service
meedoen join
meegaan accompany (go with); last (keep)
meenemen v take
meer n lake; adj more
meisje girl
meneer Mr.
menstruatie period
menstruatiepijn menstrual cramps
menukaart menu
mes knife
met with
metaal metal
meten measure
metro subway [underground BE]
metrostation subway [underground BE] station
meubels furniture
Mevrouw Mrs.; madam
middag afternoon
middernacht midnight
migraine migraine
mijn mine
minder less
minibar mini-bar
minimum minimum
minuut minute
mis mass
misschien maybe

misselijk nauseous
misselijkheid nausea
mist fog
misverstand misunderstanding
mobiel cell [mobile BE] phone
modern contemporary
moe tired
moeilijk difficult
moeras swamp
moeten must
mogelijk possible
mogen v can
mok mug
molen windmill
mond mouth
monteur mechanic
mooi beautiful
morgen tomorrow
moskee mosque
motor engine
motorboot motorboat
motorfiets motorcycle
mountainbike mountain bike
mouw sleeve
muggenbeet mosquito bite
munt coin
museum museum
muur wall
muziek music

N

na after
naaien sew
naam n name
naar to
naast next to
nacht night
nachtapotheek all-night pharmacy
nachtclub night club
nagel nail
nagelsalon nail salon
nagelvijl nail file
nagesynchroniseerd dubbed
nat wet
nationaliteit nationality

natuur nature
natuurpad nature trail
natuurreservaat nature reserve
Nederlands Dutch (language)
Nederlanders Dutch (people)
nee no
neerzetten put
nek neck
nemen v take
netnummer area code
netwerk network
neus nose
niemand nobody
nier kidney
niet do not; not
niet-EU-ingezetenen non-EU-citizens
niet-roken non-smoking
niets nothing
nieuw new
nieuws news
Nieuw-Zeeland New Zealand
nodig necessary
nodig hebben need
nog adv still
non-stop non-stop
noodgeval emergency
noodrem emergency brake
nooduitgang emergency exit
nooit never
noord north
normaal normal; regular (gas)
nu now
nul zero
nummer number
nylon nylon

O

ochtend morning
of or
ogenblik moment
oké OK
olie oil
om at (time)

omdat because
omhelzen hug
omleiding detour [diversion BE]
onbeleefd rude
onbeperkt unlimited
onbevoegd unauthorized
onder under
ondertiteld subtitled
onderzoek examination
ondiep shallow
ongelijk uneven (ground)
ongelooflijk incredible
ongeluk accident
ongeveer about (approximately)
onschuldig innocent
ontbijt breakfast
ontdooien defrost
onthouden remember
ontmoeten meet
ontmoetingsplaats meeting place [point BE]
ontruimen vacate (room)
ontsteken infect
ontsteking inflammation
ontstopper plunger
onttrekken v extract
ontvangen receive
ontvangstcentrum reception center
ontwikkelen develop
ontwrichten dislocate
onvergezeld unaccompanied
onze our
onzin nonsense
oog eye
ook also
oom uncle
oor ear
oorbellen earrings
oordruppels ear drops
oorlogsmonument war memorial
oorpijn earache
oost east
op on
opdienen serve
open adj open
openbaar public

opendoen v open (window)
openen v open
openingstijden office hours
openlucht adj outdoor
openmaken open
opera opera
operatie operation
opgezet swollen
ophalen v pick up
oplossen dissolve
opnemen withdraw (money)
oppas babysitter
oppassen caution; beware
oprit entrance ramp (highway)
oproep call
opruiming clearance; sale
opslaan save (computer)
opstaan stand up
opstijgen take off (plane)
opvullen fill up
opticien optician
opwarmen v warm
organiseren organize
origineel original
orkest orchestra
oud old
oudere senior citizens
ouders parents
ovaal oval
oven oven
over about
overbagage excess luggage [baggage BE]
overdekt indoor
overgeven v vomit
overhemd shirt (men's)
overstappen v change (bus)
oversteken v cross
overtocht crossing

P

paar pair
paard horse

paardenrenbaan horsetrack
paardrijden horseback riding
paars purple
pad path
pak suit
pakket package [parcel BE]
paleis palace
panorama panorama
pantoffels slippers
paracetamol acetaminophen [paracetamol BE]
parasol umbrella (sun) [sunshade BE]
paraplu umbrella (rain)
parel pearl
park park
parkeer en reis park and ride
parkeerdienst valet service
parkeergarage parking garage [car park BE]
parkeermeter parking meter
parkeerplaats parking lot [car park BE]
parkeerplek parking space
parkeerbon parking ticket
parkeerverbod no parking
parkeren parking
particulier private
parttime part time
paskamer fitting room
paspoort passport
passagier passenger
passen try on (clothes)
patiënt n patient
pauze intermission
paviljoen pavilion
pech breakdown (car)
pedicure pedicure
pen pen
penicilline penicillin
pensioen retirement [pension BE]

pension guesthouse
per per
per expres express mail
periode period
persen v press
personeel staff
persoon person
picknick picnic
pijn n pain
pijn hebben v hurt
pijnlijk sore
pijp pipe
pil pill
PIN PIN
pincet tweezers
pizzeria pizzeria
plaats place (location); seat (on train, etc.)
plaatselijk local
plak slice
plan plan
plant n plant
planten v plant
plastic plastic
plat flat
platina platinum
plein square
pleister bandage [plaster BE]
plezier fun
plug plug
polikliniek health clinic
politie police
politiebureau police station
polyester polyester
pomp pump
pond pound
populair popular
porselein porcelain
portemonnee wallet
portie portion
post n mail
posten v mail
postkantoor post office
posttarief postage
postwissel money order
postzegel n stamp
pot pot
praktijk practice
praten talk

prepaidkaart prepaid phone card
pretpark amusement park
prijs price
prijsverlaging discount
prima fine (good)
primus kerosene stove
privé private
probleem problem
proces-verbaal police report
proeven v taste
programma program
proost cheers
pub pub
publiek public
pyjama pajamas

R

raam window
raadplegen consult
racket racket (tennis)
rapport report
reactie reaction
recept prescription
receptie reception
receptionist receptionist
recht straight
rechts right (direction)
rechtstreeks adj direct
reddingsboot life boat
reddingsgordel life preserver [belt BE]
reddingsvest life jacket
reduceren reduce
reformproducten health food
reformwinkel health food store
regen n rain
regenen v rain
regenjas raincoat
relatie relationship
reis trip
reisbureau travel agency
reischeque traveler's check [cheque BE]
reisgids tour guide
reisorganisator tour operator

reisziekte motion sickness [travel sickness BE]
reizen travel
rekening bill
rem brake
renbaan racetrack [race course BE]
rennen run
renovatie renovation
reparatie n repair
repareren v repair
reserveren v reserve
reservering reservation
reserveringsbalie reservation desk
reservoir reservoir
restaurant restaurant
restauratiewagen dining car (train)
retourtje round-trip [return BE] ticket
richting direction
riem belt
rietje straw
rij line [queue BE]
rijbaan lane
rijbewijs driver's license
rijden drive
rijstrook lane
ring ring
ritssluiting zipper
rivier river
roeiboot rowboat
roeien row
roestvrij staal stainless steel
route route
rok skirt
roken v smoke; smoking section (restaurant)
rokerszone smoking area
rolstoel wheelchair
rolstoelopgang wheelchair ramp
roltrap escalator
roman novel
romantisch romantic
rond round (shape); around (direction)
rondleiding guided tour

rondvaart boat trip
röntgenfoto x-ray
roomservice room service
roos rose
rotonde traffic circle [roundabout BE]
rots rock
route route
roze pink
rug back (body part)
rugby rugby
rugpijn backache
rugzak backpack
ruilen exchange
ruimte space
rusten v rest
ruïne ruins
rustgebied rest area
rustig quiet

S

's avonds in the evening
's middags p.m.
's morgens a.m.
sms'en v text messaging
saai boring
sandalen sandals
satijn satin
sauna sauna
schaakspel chess
schaal scale
schaar scissors
schaatsen n skates; v ice-skating
schade damage
schadeclaim insurance claim
schaduw shade
schattig cute
scheerapparaat razor
scheerkwast shaving brush
scheermesje razor blade
scheerzeep shaving cream
scheiden divorce
schep shovel
scheren shave
scherp sharp
scheuren tear (muscle)

schilderij painting
schip ship
schoen shoe
schoenenwinkel shoe store
schoenmaker shoe repair
schok shock
schoon clean
schoonmaakmiddelen cleaning supplies
Schotland Scotland
schouder shoulder
schrijven write
schroevendraaier screwdriver
seks sex
selecteren choose
seminar seminar
servet napkin
shampoo shampoo
sieraden jewelry
siertegel decorative tile
sigaar cigar
sigarenwinkel tobacconist
sigaret cigarette
single single (person)
sjaal scarf
slaapkamer bedroom
slaappil sleeping pill
slaapwagen sleeping car [sleeper car BE]
slaapzak sleeping bag
slabbetje bib
slager butcher
slagveld battle site
slapeloosheid insomnia
slapen sleep
slecht bad
slechts only
slechthorend hearing impaired
slechtziend visually impaired
sleutel key
sleutelkaart key card
sleutelring key ring
slijter liquor store [off-licence BE]
slot n lock
sluiten v close

smaak n taste
smal narrow
smaragd emerald
snackbar snack bar
snel fast
snelheid speed
snelheidslimiet speed limit
snelweg highway [motorway BE]
sneeuw n snow
sneeuwen v snow
snijwond n cut
snoepwinkel candy store [confectioner BE]
snorkelen snorkle
sokken socks
soms sometimes
soort kind (type)
sorry sorry
soulmuziek soul music
souvenir souvenir
souvenirgids souvenir guide
souvenirwinkel souvenir store
spaarrekening savings account
spatel spatula
speciaal special
specialist specialist
speelgoed toy
speelgoedwinkel toy store
speelhal arcade
speeltuin playground
spelen play
spellen v spell
spelletje game
spiegel mirror
spier muscle
spijkerbroek jeans
spijkerstof denim
spitsuur rush hour
spons sponge
spoor platform
sport sport
sportwinkel sporting goods store
sportvereniging sports club

spreken speak
spreekkamer doctor's office [surgery BE]
spullen things
staal steel
staan stand
staanplaats standing room
stad town
stadhuis town hall
stadion stadium
stadscentrum downtown area
stadsplattegrond town map
stadsplein town square
standaard standard
standby-ticket stand-by ticket
starten v start
stadion stadium
standbeeld statue
station train [railway BE] station
steegje alley
steek bite (insect)
steelpan saucepan
steil steep
stelen steal
stempelen stamp
steriele oplossing sterilizing solution
sterk strong
sterling zilver sterling silver
steward flight attendant
stijf stiff
stijl n style
stilist stylist
stoep sidewalk [pavement BE]
stof fabric
stofzuiger vacuum cleaner
stomerij dry cleaner
stomen v steam
stopcontact electrical outlet
stoppen stop
stoplicht traffic light
storen disturb

straat street
strand beach
strandboulevard seafront
strandmeester lifeguard (beach)
streek region
strijken v iron
strijkijzer n iron
strippenkaart bus ticket
stroom stream (flow); electricity (power)
stroomversnelling rapids
stropdas n tie
student student
studeren study
stuifmeelgehalte pollen count
stuk piece
stylen v style
sufheid drowsiness
suikerpatiënt diabetic
sun-block sun-block cream
super premium (gas) [super BE]
supermarkt supermarket
surfplank surfboard
sweatshirt sweatshirt
symbool symbol
symptoom symptom
synagoge synagogue
synthetisch synthetic

T

T-shirt T-shirt
tv TV
taai tough
taalcursus language course
taalgids phrase book
tabak tobacco
tablet tablet
tafel table
takelwagen tow truck
tampon tampon
tand tooth
tandarts dentist
tandartspraktijk dental office

tandenborstel toothbrush
tandpasta toothpaste
tapijt carpet
tas bag
taxi taxi
taxistandplaats taxi stand [rank BE]
te too
team team
techniek engineering
teen toe
tegel tile
tegenover opposite
te kauwen chewable
tekenen v sign (signature)
tekst n text
telefoneren v call (phone)
telefonist telephone operator
telefoon telephone
telefoongesprek phone call
telefoongids phone directory
telefoonkaart phone card
telefoonnummer phone number
telefoonzuil pay phone
temperatuur temperature
tenger petite
tenminste at least
tennis tennis
tennisbaan tennis court
tent tent
tentharing tent peg
tentstok tent pole
terminal terminal
terugbetaling v refund
terugbrengen v return (thing)
terugkomen v return (person)
terwijl while
theater theater
theelepel teaspoon
thermometer thermometer

thermosfles thermos
thuis home
tijd time
tijdschrift magazine
tin pewter
tint tint
tissue tissue
toebehoren belong
toegang access; admission
toegangsprijs admission charge
toestaan v permit
tourist tourist
toeristische rondrit sightseeing tour
toernooi tournament
toeslag surcharge
toestel extension (phone)
toezicht supervision
toilet restroom [toilet BE]
toiletpapier toilet paper
tol toll
tolhuisje toll booth
tolk interpreter
tolweg toll road
toneelstuk play (theater)
tonen v show
tong tongue
toren tower
tot until
touringcar long-distance bus
touw rope
traditioneel traditional
tram tram
trap stairs
trein train
trekken pull
trottoir sidewalk [pavement BE]
trouwen marry
trui sweater
tuin garden
tumor tumor
tunnel tunnel
tussen between
twaalf uur 's middags noon [midday BE]
tweedehandswinkel secondhand store

tweede klas economy class
tweepersoonskamer double room

U

u you (formal)
uit from (destination); out (general)
uitchecken check out
uitgaan go out
uitgids entertainment guide
uitgang n exit
uitgeput exhausted
uitgeven spend
uitgezonderd except
uitkijkpunt vantage point, overlook
uitkleden undress
uitloggen log off
uitnodigen v invite
uitrit exit
uitrusting equipment
uitslag rash
uitsluitend exclusively
uitspreken pronounce
uitstappen get off
uitstekend terrific
uitverkocht sold out
uitzetten turn off
uitzicht view
uur hour

V

vaak adv frequent
vacature vacancy
vakantie vacation [holiday BE]
vakantiehuisje cottage
valhelm helmet
vallei valley
vallen v fall
valuta currency
vanavond tonight
vandaag today
vasthouden v hold
vast menu fixed-price menu
vechten v fight
veerboot ferry

veganist vegan
vegen wipe, sweep (clean)
vegetariër n vegetarian
vegetarisch
adj vegetarian
veilig safe
veiligheid safety
veiligheidsgordel
seat belt
veiligheidsspeld
safety pin
veilig voor kinderen
childproof
veld field
ventilator n fan
ver far
verband bandage
verbazingwekkend
amazing
verbeteren improve
verbinding connection
verbinding maken
connect
verbinding verbreken
disconnect
verboden prohibited
verboden toegang
keep out
verbreken disconnect
verdieping floor (level in
building)
verdovingsmiddel
anesthetic
verdrinken drown
verdwaald lost
vereist required
Verenigde Staten U.S.
verf paint
vergadering meeting
vergaderruimte meeting
room
vergeten forget
vergoeden v refund
vergoeding n refund
vergunning permit
vergroten enlarge
verhuizen move
verhuren rent out
verjaardag birthday
verkeerd wrong
verkeer traffic

verkeersovertreding
traffic violation
[offence BE]
verkeersvrij gebied
pedestrian zone
[precinct BE]
verklaring statement
verkoop sale
verkopen sell
verkoudheid cold (flu)
verkrachting rape
verlamming paralysis
verliezen lose
verloofd engaged
(marriage)
verloofde fiance
verloren lost
vermaken alter
verminderen reduce
verontschuldigen
apologize
verpleegster nurse
verplicht mandatory
verrekken strain
(muscle)
verrekijker binoculars
vers fresh
verschonen change
(baby)
verschuldigd zijn owe
versie version
versnapering
refreshment
versnelling gear
versperd blocked
verstellen mend
(clothes)
verstopt blocked
verstuiken twist (ankle)
versturen send (general);
mail (mail)
vertalen translate
vertaler translator
vertaling translation
vertellen tell
vertraagd delayed
vertraging delay
vertrek departures
(airport)
vertrekgate departure
gate

vertrekken v leave
vervaldatum expiration
[expiry BE] date
vervangen replace
vervangingsonderdeel
replacement part
vervelend unpleasant
verven v paint
vervoer transport
verwarming heat
[heating BE]
verwijderen remove
(general); delete
(computer)
verwonden injure
verzekering insurance
verzekeringsbewijs
insurance card
[certificate BE]
verziend far-sighted
[long-sighted BE]
videospelletje video
game
vierkant square
vies dirty
vijver pond
vinden find
vinger finger
vissen fishing
visitekaartje business
card
visum visa
vitrine display case
vlek stain
vlieg n fly
vliegen v fly
vliegtuig airplane
vliegveld airport
vlo flea
vlooienmarkt flea
market
vlucht flight
vluchtinformatie flight
information
vluchtnummer flight
number
vochtig damp
vochtinbrengende crème
moisturizer
voeden feed
voedsel food

voedselvergiftiging food
poisoning
voelen feel
voertuig vehicle
voet foot
voetbal soccer [football
BE]
voetganger pedestrian
voetgangersgebied
traffic-free zone
voetgangersover
steekplaats
pedestrian crossing
voetpad footpath
vogel bird
vol full
volgen follow
volgende next
volleybal volleyball
voltage voltage
volwassene adult
voor before (time)
voorbeeld example
voorbehoedsmiddel
contraceptive
voordat before
voorkant front
voorrang right of way
voorrang verlenen yield
[give way BE]
voorruit windshield
[windscreen BE]
voorstellen introduce
(person); suggest
(subject)
voorstelling performance
voortreffelijk superb
voorzichtig careful
vorige adj last
vork fork
vorm shape
vrachtwagen truck
[lorry BE]
vragen ask
vreemd strange
vreselijk terrible
vriend friend (male);
boyfriend
vriendelijk friendly
vriendin friend (female);
girlfriend

vrij free (no charge); vacant (unoccupied)
vroeg early
vrouw woman; wife
vrouwelijk female
vuilnis trash [rubbish BE]
vuilniszak trash bag
vullen fill
vulling filling
vuur fire
vuurtoren lighthouse
VVV tourist office

W

waar where (location); true (accurate)
waarde value
waardevol valuable
waarschuwing warning
wachten wait
wachtkamer waiting room
wachtwoord password
wagentje cart [trolley BE]
wagon car
wakker maken wake (someone)
Wales Wales
wandelen walking (general); hiking (on trail)
wandelpad walkway; trail (nature)
wandelroute walking route
wandeluitrusting hiking gear
wanneer when
warenhuis department store
warme bron hot spring
wasbaar washable
wasknijper peg
wasmachine washing machine
wasmiddel detergent
wassen wash

wasserette laundromat [launderette BE]
wasserij laundry service
wastafel sink
wat what
water water
waterski's water skis
waterskiën waterskiing
waterdicht waterproof
waterval waterfall
wedden bet
wedstrijd contest (general); game (sport)
weduwe widowed (female)
weduwnaar widowed (male)
week week
weekdag weekday
weekend weekend
weekendtarief weekend rate
weer weather
weerbericht weather forecast
weg n road; adv away
wegen weigh
wegenkaart road map
wegwerpbaar disposable
weiland field
weinig few
wekdienst wake-up call service
wekker alarm clock
welke which
welkom welcome
wenkbrauw eyebrow
wens wish
werk n work
werkeloos unemployed
werken v work
wesp wasp
west west
wie who
wieg crib [child's cot BE]
wielerwedstrijd cycling race
wielklem clamp

wij we
wijngaard vineyard
wijnkaart wine list
wijnproeven wine tasting
wijzigen v change
wind wind
winderig windy
windjack windbreaker
windmolen windmill
windsurfen windsurfing
winkel store
winkelbediende shop assistant
winkelcentrum shopping mall [centre BE]
winkelen v shopping
winkelmandje shopping basket
winkelplattegrond store guide [directory BE]
winkelwagentje shopping cart [trolley BE]
wisselen exchange
wisselgeld change
wisselkantoor currency exchange office
wisselkoers exchange rate
wit white
wol wool
wonen live
woonerf residential zone
woordenboek dictionary
worden become

Z

zakdoek handkerchief
zaken business
zakencentrum business district
zaklantaarn flashlight [torch BE]
zand sand
zebrapad crosswalk [zebra crossing BE]
zee sea
zeep soap

zeespiegel sea level
zeeziek seasick
zeggen say
zekeringkast fuse box
zeldzaam rare
zeker sure
zelfbediening self-service
zelfgemaakt homemade
zelfstandig self-employed
zetpil suppository
ziek sick [ill BE]
ziekenhuis hospital
ziektekostenverzekering health insurance
zien see
zijde silk
zilver silver
zinsnede phrase
zitplaats seat
zitten sit
zoet sweet
zon sun
zonder without
zonnebaden sunbathe
zonnebrand sunburn
zonnebrandcrème sunscreen
zonnebril sunglasses
zonnesteek sunstroke
zout n salt; adj salty
zuid south
zuigfles baby bottle
zuivel dairy
zuivelproducten dairy products
zuiver pure
zuurstof oxygen
zwaar heavy
zwanger pregnant
zwelling swelling
zwembad swimming pool
zwembroek swimming trunks
zwemmen swimming
zwempak swimsuit
zwemvest life jacket

INDEX

Berlitz pocket guide

BRUGES & GHENT

Eighth Edition 2018

Editor: Sian Marsh
Author: Jack Messenger and Brigitte Lee
Head of Production: Rebeka Davies
Picture Editor: Tom Smyth
Cartography Update: Carte
Update Production: Apa Digital
Photography Credits: Alamy 34; Bruges
Tourism 54; Chris Coe/Apa Publications 58,
69, 73, 76, 83, 96; Dreamstime 84; Fotolia 50,
64, 67, 79; Getty Images 1, 17; Glyn Genin/
Apa Publications 4TC, 4MC, 4ML, 4TL, 5TC,
5MC, 5M, 5MC, 5M, 6L, 6R, 7, 7R, 11, 26, 29,
31, 33, 37, 38, 41, 45, 47, 60, 63, 75, 88, 89, 90,
95, 99, 100; imageBROKER/REX/Shutterstock
56; iStock 20, 24, 42, 49, 92; Jerry Dennis/
Apa Publications 5T, 87; Public domain 12,
15; Shutterstock 81; Toerisme Brugge /Jan
D'Hondt 93; Tony Halliday/Apa Publications
19, 52, 71
Cover Picture: Shutterstock

Distribution
UK, Ireland and Europe: Apa Publications
(UK) Ltd; sales@insightguides.com
United States and Canada: Ingram
Publisher Services; ips@ingramcontent.com
Australia and New Zealand: Woodslane;
info@woodslane.com.au
Southeast Asia: Apa Publications (SN) Pte;
singaporeoffice@insightguides.com
Worldwide: Apa Publications (UK) Ltd;
sales@insightguides.com

**Special Sales, Content Licensing
and CoPublishing**
Insight Guides can be purchased in bulk
quantities at discounted prices. We can
create special editions, personalised jackets
and corporate imprints tailored to your
needs. sales@insightguides.com;
www.insightguides.biz

Contact us
Every effort has been made to provide
accurate information in this publication,
but changes are inevitable. The publisher
cannot be responsible for any resulting loss,
inconvenience or injury. We would appreciate
it if readers would call our attention to any
errors or outdated information. We also
welcome your suggestions; please contact
us at: berlitz@apaguide.co.uk
www.insightguides.com/berlitz